# KING ARTHUR

## A MILITARY HISTORY

# KING ARTHUR
# A MILITARY HISTORY

MICHAEL HOLMES

BLANDFORD

**A BLANDFORD BOOK**

First published in the UK 1996 by Blandford
A Cassell Imprint
Cassell Plc, Wellington House,
125 Strand, London WC2R 0BB



First published in paperback 1998



Distributed in the United States by Sterling Publishing Co., Inc.
387 Park Avenue South, New York, NY 10016–8810

British Library Cataloguing-in-Publication Data
A catalogue entry for this title is available from the British Library

ISBN 0–7137–2739–X

Typeset by York House Typographic Ltd, London
Printed and bound in Great Britain by Creative Print & Design (Wales), Ebbw Vale

To
Honorine

# Contents

# List of Maps

# Acknowledgements

MY MAIN aim in this book has been to argue that Arthur, the last High King of Britain, was not only a real, as distinct from a legendary, character but also a man who had a profound influence on the development of the history of England and, consequently, of the world. In this, I have been much influenced by the works of Professor Leslie Alcock and the late Dr John Morris and my thanks are due to both.

I have attempted to coordinate evidence from as many diverse reliable sources as possible, with the objective of producing a view of events in Britain around the year 500 which supports both the existence and the importance of Arthur. Some of the arguments used are based on the texts of Gildas and Nennius, and I have used the translations of the originals provided in *The History from the Sources* published by Phillimore. A translation of *The Anglo-Saxon Chronicle* taken from the Everyman edition has been used throughout. Other texts consulted are listed in the Bibliography. Special thanks are due to Mr S. E. Rigold, whose two papers on the location of Domnoc in East Anglia have been used as key elements in the argument presented in Chapter 8. Needless to say, responsibility for any of the deductions drawn from any of the sources is mine alone.

In addition, my thanks are due to my sons and daughter-in-law, Andrew, Christopher and Katherine, for providing advice and a valuable forum for discussion. Finally and above all, my thanks are due to my wife, Honorine, without whose encouragement and support this book could never have been written.

# Acknowledgements

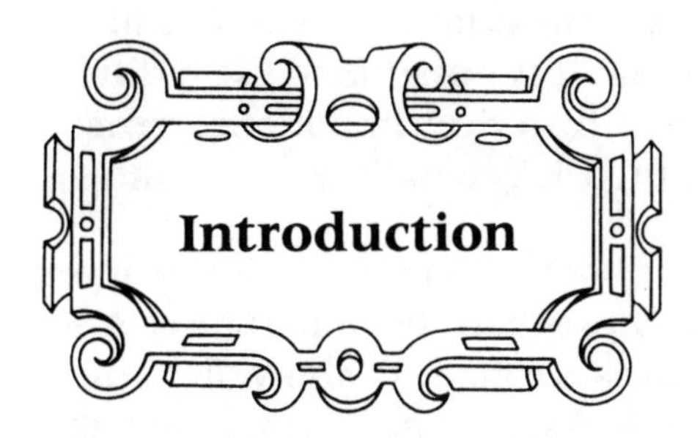

# Introduction

THERE HAVE been many books written on the subject of King Arthur but the great majority have concentrated on either the mythical or the legendary aspects, both of which were first developed in prose form in the twelfth century. These stories have one theme in common: they show the legendary Arthur as a great king and military leader. The real Arthur may well have been as great a man as the legend depicts. However, the search for the real man, the historical character, was not attempted to any major extent until the present century. In this connection two important works were published some 20 years ago. The first, *Arthur's Britain*, by Professor Leslie Alcock, appeared in 1971 and the second, *The Age of Arthur*, by Dr John Morris, in 1973. Both accept Arthur as an important historical character living around 500. Professor Alcock limits Arthur's importance to the military sphere and regards his political effect as negligible. Dr Morris, on the other hand, sees him as both a military leader and someone who exerted great influence on British history as a whole.

Neither has convinced every historian that Arthur played a unique role in repelling the Anglo-Saxon invasion of this island. In 1986 Dr J. N. L. Myres, in his book *The English Settlements*, asserted:

> The fact is that there is no contemporary or near-contemporary evidence for Arthur playing any decisive part in these events at all. No figure on the borderline of history and mythology has wasted more of the historian's time ... But if we add anything to the bare statement that Arthur may have lived and fought the Saxons, we pass at once from history to romance.

Although Dr Myres's comment on the lack of contemporary evidence has substance, the evidence of Alcock and Morris supporting the importance of Arthur is impressive. This makes the almost total rejection of their views by Dr Myres all the more surprising. My own attitude to the Arthurian matter is more in accord with that of Alcock and Morris, but it would be difficult to provide more than a limited number of new facts to support their arguments since, taken together, they examine most of the components in this history. However, it has become apparent that it is possible to use a different approach to the problem of Arthur's historical importance posed by such divergent attitudes. This approach generally extends the views of Alcock and Morris.

At the outset, this book rejects any appeal to legend or myth in order to support Arthur's existence or importance. A few very brief references to these sources are made to show, first, the inadequacies of the legend in the historical sense and, second, how the historical fact has, occasionally, affected the legend. Nowhere has the legend been presented as a support of historical fact.

The approach adopted supports the importance of Arthur's place in history through an examination of the generally accepted 'broad-brush' overview of the history of western Europe during Arthur's time. This involves the comparison of events in Gaul and Britain during the period covered by the Germanic invasions of both Roman provinces. The comparison shows that it is reasonable to identify the outcome with Arthur's intervention. This plan also involves an appreciation of the Celtic, Germanic and Roman backgrounds of the leaders of defence and attack, in particular Arthur in Britain and Clovis in Gaul. Such backgrounds provide possibly the best, if not the only, method of assessing the reactions of such leaders to the events they had to face.

In both of these two themes, overview and background, military matters play a major role. This is a result of the emphasis placed by the historical records on battles won and lost in those early years. It is a matter of well-accepted record that in the period before and during Arthur's life these two dioceses of the western Roman Empire (the division has no ecclesiastical significance), Britain and Gaul, were subjected to attack after attack by barbarian tribes from the north and east of Europe. Apart from their interest in the growth and spread of Christianity, contemporary historians in the fifth and sixth centuries concentrated their attention upon these attacks.

When making the comparison between the historical sequences in Britain and Gaul during the Germanic invasions, it is unfortunately true that there is much less information available on the former. This is due to the quality of the material provided by near-contemporary writers in Britain and Gaul. Bishop Gregory of Tours is far more informative in his *Historia Francorum* (*History of the Franks*) than is Gildas in his work *De Excidio et Conquestu Britanniae* (*On the Ruin of Britain*). Gildas is more concerned with castigating the leaders of Britain for their moral failings than with providing historical facts. Additional information is, however, available from Nennius's *Historia Brittonum* (*History of the British*), the *Annales Cambriae* (*Welsh Annals*) and *The Anglo-Saxon Chronicle*, although all these sources were compiled some three or four centuries after the invasions. Even so, the records are particularly valuable for the simple reason that their writers must have known more about their recent history than we ever can. They completed their work between the sixth and ninth centuries and were closer to Arthurian times by more than 1,000 years than we are. There are a few cases where the evidence is contradictory, and here efforts have been made to choose the correct version. In the event it proved necessary to correct only one obvious error in Gildas and one date in *The Anglo-Saxon Chronicle*.

Following this plan, it has been possible for an assessment to be made of the relative merits of leaders of the attack and defence in the invasions of these two Roman dioceses. As indicated earlier, the background influences play a major role. In particular, the expertise of the British leaders used in the defence of the island comes from both Celtic and Roman sources and each culture will have influenced military performance. The merit assessment may also go some way to support the records of Arthur's successes in battle, which have not been wholeheartedly accepted by many historians.

These arguments in support of Arthurian importance are strengthened by some results of modern archaeological and historical research, by philology, by reasonable estimates of human life expectancy and by the assumption that leaders of fighting men in those times would have attempted to behave as rationally and intelligently as we do, at least in planning the strategy of a military campaign.

With all these sources of information, it has proved possible to outline a sequence of events in the Anglo-Saxon invasion of Britain which can be linked with the major decisions Arthur, and his immediate predecessors, Ambrosius and Vortigern, must have made in military and political matters during their lifetimes. The sequence constructed is in agreement with all the documentary records and can be correlated with earlier and later historical data, such as, for example, the *Notitia Dignitatum*, a fifth-century army list, and the site of the first see of the East Angles. Some of the events in the sequence, taken separately, may seem to have a degree of uncertainty. However, their position in the sequence lends support to their accuracy when they are seen to fit well with both earlier and later events.

The British sequence can then be placed alongside the Gallic sequence, which has firmer historical support. On the foundation of the two sequences, the exceptional and unique results of the Anglo-Saxon invasion of Britain, when compared with the outcome of the Frankish invasion of Gaul, are used to support the concept that Arthur played an important role in the history of the turbulent times around the year 500. As a consequence, the Arthurian role can be linked to the development of an Anglo-Saxon culture, relatively undisturbed by Celtic, Roman (apart from ecclesiastical) or other external influences for some 500 years. There is little doubt that this culture has had an important bearing on world history.

# The Problem of Arthur

GREAT ARTHUR, the mysterious king in times long past, has haunted the history of Britain for more than 1,000 years. Unfortunately, the real man appears, like the tip of an iceberg, in only a few ancient documents. The historical importance of the man and his achievements, the bulk of the iceberg, is certainly not revealed by these sparse records. Nevertheless, he may have held a position of great and real importance, for his stature has certainly made itself felt through the poems of bards and through the growth of legends written centuries after his death. These poems and legends, although extolling the theme of Arthurian greatness, have perhaps only exposed an imaginary base to the iceberg and have diverted attention away from the real man.

As a consequence, of all the books on the subject of Arthur in modern times, most have taken the position that the history of Arthur is in fact the history of the literature. That is to say, their main theme is directed towards an examination of the Arthurian legend as revealed by authors, both English and Continental, writing between the twelfth and fifteenth centuries – at least some 600 years after the generally agreed period of Arthur's life. This is not surprising, for the legend in the hands of the medieval writers makes a wonderful series of stories which have captured the imagination of readers throughout Europe and the English-speaking world.

The Matter of Britain, as the Arthurian saga became known, may have been developed using very meagre historical records, supplemented by bardic poems, but undoubtedly the skill of the superb masters of English, French and German literature in medieval times played a major role. So successful were these writers that they inspired archaeological searches for sites which could be linked with the man behind the legend. These searches (which will be described in greater detail later) were largely unsuccessful in discovering any facts relating to Arthur's real life. Consequently, apart from generating a general interest in the sites, the searches played little part in diverting attention from a heroic legendary king to an ordinary mortal leader who, despite his achievements, in the end did not prevent the final success of the Anglo-Saxon invasion.

To reiterate, the present book is not concerned with the history of the literature. Its objective is rather to pursue a search for the real or historical Arthur, based not on the legend but primarily on the very limited contemporary, or near-contemporary, evidence and on the 'broad-brush' view of the history of the times around 500. These times were particularly critical for the inhabitants of western Europe. The Roman Empire in the west was in decline and attacks on Britain and Gaul were increasing in intensity. The Anglo-Saxons were moving against Britain and the Franks against Gaul. These nationwide trends are well authenticated and the invasion patterns in both countries are known in broad terms.

The sparse Arthurian documentation can possibly be used in conjunction with the invasion patterns in the fifth and sixth centuries to reveal the stature of the true Arthur, as distinct from the imaginary mass of the iceberg. This approach will be used in the expectation that his achievements could perhaps be shown to be so important that the fame of the legendary king would be equalled if not overshadowed by that of the real man.

Before starting to consider the methods needed to pursue the objective, it is necessary to show that the legends cannot be safely used as a source of reliable history, even though they have given rise to archaeological investigations in the search for Arthurian fact. In order to make it quite clear that the legends are of little, if any, value in the search for the historical Arthur, it is therefore appropriate to examine briefly their structure and credibility and their links with archaeology.

The stories of Arthur's adventures and those of his knights started to be told in England and in France around 1100 and spread throughout Europe in the Middle Ages. They are now well known in all the English-speaking world. Recently a musical play entitled *Camelot*, based on Arthur and his court, received wide acclaim on both sides of the Atlantic. The popularity of the stories reached a peak in medieval times, when they were first written in the forms which have survived to the present day. As a consequence, the background to the stories is medieval, and certainly does not correspond to the times of the Anglo-Saxon invasion some six centuries earlier. The stories do, however, match lifestyles of authors such as Geoffrey of Monmouth, Chrétien de Troyes and Sir Thomas Malory.

A colourful picture is presented of Arthur's birth, life and death, superimposed on the image of life at a royal court in the Middle Ages. The chivalry of Arthur's knights and the pageantry of tournaments also play a part in sustaining the reader's interest. Within this framework there are two main themes, one secular and the other religious. The secular theme is concerned with Arthur's conquest of most of the western Roman Empire, culminating almost in the subjugation of Rome itself. This outcome is prevented only by treachery at home, led by Medraut and ending in the death of both Arthur and Medraut at a final climactic battle. This theme is complemented by a religious cycle of stories which contain strong magical and some pagan elements. In this cycle almost the whole of Arthur's knightly company is dispersed in order to search for the Holy Grail, the cup used by Christ at the Last Supper. As the stories grew in popularity, others were written using the concept of the Round Table, a meeting place at court for the knights where there was no order of precedence. From there the knights rode out to do good, to seek adventure and to rescue ladies in distress.

It became progressively more difficult to accept the legends as history. First, the magical and supernatural elements in the stories were recognized for what they were and their inclusion cast doubt on the authenticity of the rest. Subsequently, some allegedly historical facts mentioned in the stories were seen to be untenable. For example, the concept of a British king who took his armies in a victorious campaign almost to the gates of Rome in the latter years of the fifth century, as one author, Geoffrey of Monmouth, claimed, was clearly false. It was gradually realized that none of the stories written around these themes matched the violent history of the barbaric invasions of the Roman Empire which occurred around the year 500.

As a result of these doubts, the credibility of Arthur as a historical character was severely diminished. Consequently, for modern readers, the whole cycle of tales has become little more than a delightful legend and, although given a somewhat vague position in history within the period of the first Anglo-Saxon invasions, Arthur is usually better remembered today as a figure belonging to the realm of fairy-tales than as a king of Britain in ancient times.

This was not always the case, particularly at the time when the Arthurian literature was created in the twelfth century. Then the stories were widely accepted as a true history of Britain around the year 500. However, there was, even in early medieval times, one serious historian who not only felt that Arthur played an important role in history but also realized that the records of his true greatness were being obscured by the legend. William of Malmesbury knew that poets and writers had taken charge of Arthur's image and had turned his life into a fictional legend which fitted well with the contemporary romantic traditions of chivalry. In his book *Gesta Regum* (*History of the Kings*) he wrote: 'This is that Arthur of whom modern Welsh fancy raves. Yet he ought to be remembered in authentic history rather than in idle fiction, for he long preserved the sinking state.' Clearly, William accepted the existence of Arthur as a historical character whose actions were important in successfully opposing the Anglo-Saxon invaders for many years, even though, in the end, Arthur's Britain was destroyed by Anglo-Saxon England. At the same time, William firmly separates the historical Arthur from the man whose adventures dominated much of the romantic literature of his time.

Although some modern historians accept William's view of Arthur's existence, they are not, at the same time, prepared to support his assessment of Arthur's importance. They take the position that, at best, Arthur was perhaps a minor chieftain or tribal leader who lived around the year 500 and had very little influence, if any at all, on the momentous history of the Anglo-Saxon conquest. Proponents of this view would possibly argue that the reputation of such a man had been magnified out of all proportion by the extremely skilled writers of historical fiction in medieval times between the twelfth and fifteenth centuries.

In a central position, other historians take an agnostic attitude, believing that present knowledge is inadequate to reach a firm conclusion on the stature of Arthur in history, and it must certainly be admitted that reliable information is somewhat scarce.

Of those in a final category who incline to William's view of Arthur's importance, the most committed insist that Arthur played a key role in the history of Britain and England; this is also the conclusion reached in the present book. However, whether or not Arthur played a major part, it is certainly true that at this particular time, around the year 500, the future of the land was being decided for the next 500 years at least, and perhaps for very much longer.

The reasons for these diverse opinions arise as a reflection of the lack of firm information relating to the period of Arthur's lifetime, towards the end of the first century of the Dark Ages in Britain. It is now generally accepted that the Dark Ages stretch from 410 to 871, from the abandonment of Britain by Rome to the accession of Alfred. This would place Arthur's life midway between 410 and the accession of Raedwald, King of the East Angles, in 616. (The latter is best known for his association with the ship burial at Sutton Hoo near Woodbridge in Suffolk.)

The uncertainty surrounding the Dark Ages has impeded the pursuit of historical research and consequently provided a fertile field for the growth of the Arthurian story cycle which later captured the imagination of western Europe. As a result the stories exerted such a powerful influence on their readers that, as mentioned earlier, they stimulated searches in both modern and medieval times for firm evidence to support any aspect of Arthur's life or exploits.

These searches were archaeological and the results were inconclusive in nearly all respects. Because the searches did nothing to provide firm, unequivocal evidence of Arthur's existence, their failure, combined with lack of fully accredited records, probably influenced many historians to downgrade his historical importance. It is, however, useful to show how the story cycle gave rise to the searches, for their negative results were important in guiding historical opinion.

Three facets of the story cycle have had particular influence on the search for Arthurian fact: the locations of his birth, of the chief centre of his military activities and of his burial. Searches for these locations have been extensive, for the very meagre historical documentation of the years around 500 gives no clues. Archaeological research, both medieval and modern, has therefore been directed towards pinpointing these sites using clues based on the legend. Although such investigations would probably provide little direct information on events in Arthur's life, they might, if successful, provide some firm reference points for his career.

Some indication of the area of Britain where Arthur may have been born is provided by his name, which could be derived from the Roman family name Artorius, for he was almost certainly of Roman-Celtic descent. A region of Britain favoured by the wealthy in those times was the uplands around Gloucester and Cirencester, the Cotswolds, where the sites of many Roman villas have been found. Arthur's family may well have come from that prosperous part of the country, but no direct supporting evidence has been discovered.

The legend, however, has provided a site for the birth of Arthur and this has been precisely located in Geoffrey of Monmouth's book *Historia Regum Britanniae* (*History of the Kings of Britain*), which was written in about 1136 and became a 'best-seller' in the Middle Ages. Geoffrey claimed that his book was factual and based on 'a certain very ancient book written in the British language' which was presented to him by Walter, Archdeacon of Oxford. The source book has, however, never been found and to modern eyes Geoffrey's story is clearly closer to historical fiction than to historical fact. By the majority of less critical medieval readers, it was accepted as substantially factual and it formed the basis of two early Arthurian romances, the *Romance of Britain* by a Norman poet named Wace, which appeared in 1155, and *Britain* by Layamon, an English priest writing in the first half of the thirteenth century.

When dealing with Arthur's birthplace, Geoffrey relates how Uther Pendragon, King of Britain, had fallen in love with Ygerna, the wife of Gorlois, Duke of Cornwall, and in consequence had declared war on the Duke. Since Gorlois's army was smaller than the King's, the Duke decided to withdraw his forces into fortified castles in order to await reinforcements from Ireland. He left his wife in his castle at Tintagel, on the north coast of Cornwall, while he was besieged by Uther in a fortified camp at Dimilioc, eight kilometres (five miles) to the south-west. Geoffrey tells us that Uther's passion for Ygerna had become so intense that he determined to ask Ulfin, one of his closest friends, what he could do to satisfy his desire. Ulfin advises him that no power on earth can force an entry into the fortress of Tintagel, for 'the castle is built high above the sea, which surrounds it on all sides, and there is no other way in except that offered by a narrow isthmus of rock. Three armed soldiers could hold it against you, even if you stood there with the whole kingdom of Britain at your side.' Ulfin then suggests that the prophet Merlin may be able to help the King. Merlin is sent for and he provides a solution to the King's problem. Through magic he will change the appearance of the King, Ulfin and himself to correspond with the appearance, respectively, of Gorlois and two of his retainers. The three will then enter the fortress with no difficulty and Ygerna will receive Uther as Gorlois. The plan succeeds and Arthur is conceived. Meanwhile, the Duke has been killed in an unsuccessful sally from Dimilioc. The three intruders leave Tintagel and return to their own appearances. Finally, Uther returns to Tintagel as King, captures the castle and claims Ygerna as wife and Queen.

By modern standards this tale is pure fantasy, but it was not so regarded by the more credulous readers of medieval times. Geoffrey had in fact taken care to add as many authentic details as he could to his story. He must have been well acquainted with Tintagel, for, as his name suggests, he was probably from the West Country.

Even today the headland at Tintagel appears to be an ideal site for a castle and the narrow isthmus joining the promontory to the mainland still fits Ulfin's description exactly. The ruins of the castle are evident but, unfortunately for the legend, the records indicate that it was built in the years following 1141 by Reginald, Earl of Cornwall, the illegitimate son of Henry I. It is more than likely that Geoffrey saw the building work in progress. Later improvements and extensions were made in about 1236 by Richard, also Earl of Cornwall and younger brother of Henry III.

All the castle buildings are situated on either side of the isthmus joining the headland to the mainland, and on the headland itself a further site was investigated in 1935 (see Radford 1935). This was identified as the remains of a Celtic monastery dating from the late fifth or early sixth century. These remains may have been more in evidence in medieval times and could have given Geoffrey the idea that there was an earlier castle on the same site which could have been the birthplace of Arthur. Archaeology in those days was almost non-existent and what has now been identified as the remains of a Celtic monastery could have been mistaken for Gorlois's castle in simpler times.

There are then no firm archaeological discoveries linking Tintagel with Arthur, although the dating of the monastery makes it probable that it was there in his lifetime. If monastic tradition is to be believed, as expressed in various lives of saints written around the twelfth century, Arthur did not enjoy amicable relations with the early Church and it is not likely that he would have had any contact with the Celtic monastery at Tintagel. However, a fresh investigation of the Tintagel site was proposed in 1991 and the outcome of this is awaited with interest, although it is not expected to yield direct evidence of Arthurian occupation.

There is no firm evidence relating to the end of Arthur's life, apart from the mention of his death in battle which appears in one of the historical records. These records provide no information whatever of his burial place and the legends are equally reticent. Geoffrey of Monmouth recounts that Arthur was mortally wounded in a battle on the River Camblam in Cornwall 'and was carried off to the Isle of Avalon, so that his wounds might be attended to. He handed the crown of Britain over to his cousin Constantine ... in the year 542.' Death and burial are not mentioned, leaving a way open for future generations to believe that Arthur is sleeping, waiting only to awaken and lead his country to victory in the hour of its greatest need. Sir Thomas Malory in his great epic *Le Morte d'Arthur*, published in 1485, agrees with Geoffrey that Arthur was carried to the Isle of Avalon so that his wounds could be healed. Additionally, following early French writers, Malory tells of the journey to Avalon in a barge accompanied by many ladies. Both Malory and the French authors record final burial in a chapel, but no one indicates its location.

In Celtic myth, the Isle of Avalon lies beyond the sea to the west and is believed to be a mysterious paradise for favoured mortals after death. Clearly, it is impossible to locate such a place geographically. There have been, however, some attempts to equate Avalon with Glastonbury, and this idea probably first arose when the monks of Glastonbury Abbey announced in 1191 the results of a medieval archaeological investigation. According to Giraldus Cambrensis, they claimed to have discovered the site of Arthur's grave within the abbey precincts. It had been found between two pyramids just to the south of the Lady Chapel of the abbey. The body was identified by a lead cross within the coffin with an inscription which reads, according to the Tudor historian John Leland:

HIC IACET SEPVLTVS INCLITVS REX ARTVRIVS IN INSVLA AVALONIA

Here lies buried the famous King Arthur in the Isle of Avalon.

The cross has disappeared, but in 1607 William Camden provided in his *Britannia* what is probably a reasonably accurate drawing of it and this has permitted an analysis of the style to be made. Alcock suggests that though the lettering is certainly not sixth century, nor is it twelfth. A best estimate would be tenth century and this might imply a forger who realized that a twelfth-century inscription would be unacceptable but had no knowledge of sixth-century letter forms. On the other hand, it is known that St Dunstan reconstructed the cemetery in the tenth century and, again as Alcock suggests, he could have re-marked the grave with the lead cross. This would explain the printing and also the use of the word 'King', a title which was not ascribed to Arthur in the earliest documents.

Confidence in the monastery's claim is unfortunately diminished by the existence of at least two motives for deception by the monks. There had been a fire at the monastery a few years earlier and the monks were short of funds for the necessary repairs. With Arthur's grave inside the abbey grounds, alms could certainly be collected from pilgrims demanding to visit the burial place of so famous a king. There was also a political motive which might have been behind the discovery. The Celtic subjects in the empire of Henry II were restless and there was a belief that the young Arthur, son of Geoffrey of Anjou and Constance of Brittany, could perhaps be a reincarnation of King Arthur who would lead the Celts against the Norman king. The grave at Glastonbury containing the body of Arthur would effectively counter this belief.

With all these doubts and uncertainties, confidence in the association of Arthur with either Tintagel or Glastonbury remains very weak.

Moreover, neither association contributes in any way to belief in his importance. There is, however, one other archaeological investigation which, although yielding little direct evidence of an Arthurian link, does provide very valuable circumstantial evidence. This relates to the search for the site of Arthur's military headquarters.

The very limited early documentary evidence emphasizes Arthur's qualities as a soldier but gives no indication of the whereabouts of his military base. Once again, legend is much less reticent and Geoffrey of Monmouth places Arthur's plenary court at Caerleon, on the River Usk in south Wales. This was the Roman headquarters of the Second Legion, the Augusta, and it is possible that Geoffrey made his choice on the basis of the Roman remains to be found there: the military amphitheatre and hospital, for example.

Both Malory and the French authors of the Arthurian romances agree that the court moved from place to place in Britain, but all nominate the castle and city of Camelot as the capital of Arthur's kingdom. The name Camelot first occurs in the romance by Chrétien de Troyes entitled *Lancelot,* which postdates Geoffrey by some thirty years, and Camelot has been accepted as the location for Arthur's capital by all who are more concerned with the legend than with historical reality. Unfortunately, the romances give no indication of the precise geographical location of Camelot and any search for the real Arthur should include a search for the chief centre of his activities, whether it be a royal capital or a military headquarters.

The only early British town which, by its name alone, could be identified as Camelot is Colchester in Essex. In Roman times Colchester was known as Camulodunum and Morris (1973: 138) suggests that Camelot could be located there. The supporting arguments are based on the strategic position of Colchester between the invaders to the north in East Anglia and to the south in Kent. A British power base here might dominate both invaders' bridgeheads. In addition, Colchester's maritime links with the Continent could facilitate supply and reinforcements from Roman bases in Gaul. Neither of these arguments is conclusive.

The first suffers from the obvious danger of placing a main headquarters in such an exposed position. During the early invasion sequence, the strength of the British lay in the west and the invaders made their presence known in the east, and Colchester is near the east coast. The lines of communication between Colchester and the west would be far too long. The second argument is weakened by the fact that in 486 Clovis eliminated Roman power in northern Gaul, so preventing any possible Roman reinforcements from reaching

Arthur's forces. A case can be made for a forward base in the east but not for a capital or chief military headquarters.

There are, however, certain requirements which a military leader of the British would need around the year 500 when facing invasion of the island in both the east and south by tribes coming across the North Sea from lands around the Danish peninsula. He would need a base some distance behind the areas under direct invasion threat in order to be able to deploy his forces to the east or south as required. Such a site would also have to provide security for recruitment and training of his forces and be a safe place to withdraw his troops to for rest and recuperation after engagements on the invasion coasts.

In seaching for the actual site it is not possible to seek the 'many tower'd Camelot' of Tennyson's 'The Lady of Shalott'. Such castles were to appear in England only after another half-millennium. There were, however, alternative structures available in Britain in the Dark Ages which could fulfil most of the needs, namely the Iron Age hill-forts. Many are in the south-west and one looked very promising to the archaeologists, the fort at South Cadbury in Somerset.

The link between Castle Cadbury and Camelot was probably first made by Leland in 1542 on the basis of local folklore, supported by the discovery of Roman coins on the site. The 'castle' is a large, flat-topped hill some 20 kilometres (12 miles) south-east of Glastonbury. The top of the hill covers an area of about seven hectares (18 acres) and is large compared with other hill-forts, such as the 0.4-hectare (one-acre) site of Castle Dore in Cornwall. The top, being over 150 metres (500 feet) above sea level, commands a clear view across Somerset to Glastonbury Tor and beyond, almost to the Bristol Channel, 40 kilometres (26 miles) to the north-west. Most important of all, Cadbury is at least 80 kilometres (50 miles) to the west of the furthest Anglo-Saxon penetration at the end of the fifth century. Communications to the north-east, to the east and to the south coast were excellent, being served by two nearby Roman roads: the Fosse Way, leading through Bath and middle Britain to Lincolnshire and Norfolk, and a second road passing north of Salisbury through Silchester to London and Colchester. Both would be invaluable in providing access to the invasion coasts.

For all these reasons, the Cadbury site was examined in detail between 1966 and 1970 by a team led by Professor Alcock and many discoveries relevant to the Arthurian connection were made, although no specific indication that Arthur ever occupied the fort could be found (see Alcock 1968). Discoveries of pottery and a Germanic silver buckle on a post-Roman, pre-Saxon rampart suggested extensive refortification work around the year 500 – within Arthur's lifetime.

The layout of the hill-top would have allowed a smaller area to have been refortified, but the whole seven hectares had been included in the project, making the castle the largest site to be so treated in Britain in the fifth and sixth centuries.

According to Alcock, Castle Cadbury is exceptional in terms of size and strength of refortification among all British strongholds. He believes it unlikely that it was intended as a defended homestead or a tribal centre, and thinks it much more likely that it was a large army base. Although there is no direct evidence of Arthurian occupation, it is almost certain that the large fort was reinforced and manned by a Celtic leader around the year 500. (The Anglo-Saxons did not penetrate so far west until the middle of the seventh century.) Consequently, although the word 'Camelot' has no known existence around 500, the site at Cadbury might well have been Arthur's military headquarters.

In summary, all the archaeological evidence relating to Arthur's birth and to his grave is inconclusive and, on balance, gives little support to his existence or importance. Only the evidence from Cadbury could provide some support for his influence on history, and this possibility will be reconsidered later.

There remains another source of evidence which strongly supports both Arthur's existence and his importance but which is basically deficient in facts: the poems and stories of the Welsh bards, first handed down by word of mouth and later in written form. This writing predates the legends which developed in medieval times. In these earlier stories, the people who survived the conquering Anglo-Saxons, possibly due to the difficulties of the Welsh terrain, look back to the time when they occupied almost all the island and were led by a great hero. Sometimes the bards refer to Arthur as *'tywyssawc cat'*, leader of battle, sometimes as *'tywyssawc llu'* leader of the army, and in one poem, 'Elegy for Geraint', he is called *'amaraudur'* or emperor. It is this early tradition which led to the belief in the heroic stature of King Arthur, the central figure in the great flood of literature which burgeoned 600 years later. Although the bardic writings express very strong feelings on the subject of Arthur and certainly regarded him highly, they are the product of poets rather than historians and the former are not renowned for accurate and dispassionate judgements.

If the bards are discounted as providers of fact and the archaeological evidence is inconclusive, there remain the few historical documents, some more credible than others, which do record Arthur's name and some of his achievements. They will be considered in detail later, but though they may have been accepted as evidence of his existence, they have not been generally accepted as confirmation of his historical importance.

This brief review indicates the lack of firm evidence which perhaps accounts for the reservations of many historians mentioned earlier. It would clearly be useful if some direct documentary evidence were to be found to clear up the matter, but this is most unlikely, and to hope for new archaeological Arthurian discoveries is unrealistic. Something more is needed if the bardic view of Arthur's importance is to be accepted by either historians or informed lay readers.

Without doubt, there is an absence of strong factual evidence from a reliable historical source and this constitutes the main problem underlying any attempt to sustain the concept of Arthur's importance as a real person with a firm place in history. Failing new archaeological or documentary evidence, it is possible that the solution to this problem needs the approach, outlined earlier, which takes account of all the limited documentation available, together with the generally accepted information relating to the invasions of Britain and Gaul by tribes from the north-west of Europe.

However, the generally accepted information on the invasions does not, in the case of Britain, provide much information on individuals, and here the concern is very much related to one individual: Arthur. This is due to the fact that the period before, during and after the Anglo-Saxon conquest falls within the Dark Ages in Britain and consequently information relating to any particular individual is sometimes hard to find and, even if found, harder still to confirm. This difficulty can, nevertheless, be overcome, for there must be links between the well-known general historical trends and important individuals living in those times, even if those individuals are not named or their achievements listed in acceptable documents. An unusual trend could indicate the presence of some unnamed leader who initiated the trend. But then again, even the unusual cannot easily be identified, for after a time lapse of 1,500 years the usual is not known with any confidence.

There is even a way around this obstacle, if a country can be found with a similar historical starting point to that of Britain in the early years of the fifth century but with substantial differences at the turn of the century and during the sixth century. The divergence may then have a cause which is strongly dependent on differences in leadership in the two countries. In particular, the divergence would indicate the importance and quality of a leader, unnamed in the accepted 'broad-brush' history but named in otherwise unauthenticated documents. (Leadership qualities in those early days were perhaps much more important in guiding the destinies of small nations or tribes than in modern times, when more complex economic, political and social factors often take precedence over the abilities of any single man.) Under these circumstances, the greater the divergence between the histories of Britain and this other country, the greater the historical importance of the leaders who caused it.

It is not necessary to look far for such a country. Britain and Gaul (now France) were both Celtic countries conquered by the Romans in the first century AD and absorbed into the empire. They had similar social, religious and cultural backgrounds modified by the same conqueror and were forced to adopt the same Roman political, military and administrative structures. At the end of the fourth century, Britain and Gaul had become adjacent dioceses in the praetorian prefecture of the Gauls. In the fifth century, both dioceses were detached from imperial control and authority became vested in provincial leaders who were, at least in part, influenced by Roman traditions. Both Britain and northern Gaul were then subjected to barbarian attack from Germanic tribes beyond the imperial frontiers. These attacks occurred in the fifth century and the early years of the sixth. The responses of each province during and after the attack are known in general terms and these responses may well show the divergences that are being sought.

The names of the leaders in Britain whose qualities will be under examination can be found in reasonably reliable documents, but not in well-authenticated general history. There are only six of any consequence who are so mentioned, as distinct from the many who appear in bardic poems. They are, from the early fifth century to the first years of the sixth, Vortigern and the Elder Ambrosius, their sons, respectively Vortimer and the Younger Ambrosius, and finally Arthur and Medraut. The achievements and actions of these men will be introduced as possible causes for the generally accepted trend of the history of the Anglo-Saxon conquest over the years between 430 and 520. Leaders of the invading barbarians of comparable status to the British leaders are named in *The Anglo-Saxon Chronicle*. They are, over the same period as the British leaders, Hengist, Aelle, Cerdic and Cynric. In the years after 520 Ceawlin, Cuthulf and Aethelbert are also named by the *Chronicle* as leaders of the invaders up to the end of the sixth century. There are no recorded leaders of the British of equivalent stature in this later period for reasons which will become apparent.

The situation was different in Gaul. Reliable historians such as Gregory of Tours enabled the names of Gallic leaders to be included in authenticated history. In Gaul the two leaders named as defending the northern part of the diocese in the later fifth century are Aegidius and his son Syagrius. These two could perhaps be regarded as the last independent Roman leaders in Gaul. In the south-west of Gaul, the leaders of the western Roman Empire had already allowed the Visigoths to settle under their King Alaric II, and the Burgundians, under their leaders Gundobad and Godigisel, had settled in the upper valley of the Rhône. There was, in the late fifth century and early sixth, only one leader of the invaders of Gaul who was of any consequence, Clovis, the son of Childeric, King of the Salian Franks.

The search for, and discovery of, broad divergences in the development of England and France will be used to show and support the important place Arthur holds in the history of both Britain and England. At the same time, while there will be little probability of uncovering direct evidence relating to his personality or character, it will be much easier to identify the historical influences which must have contributed to that character.

These influences will make it possible to identify background knowledge which he, and other leaders, would almost certainly possess, gathered from history as they knew it. Such background knowledge would without doubt, and in its turn, influence action. The spread of Roman military power to Britain and Gaul would ensure that the leaders in both countries, and in neighbouring countries outside the empire, knew of advanced Roman military techniques. Knowledge of Celtic strengths and weaknesses in Britain and Gaul, and corresponding Germanic qualities in the invading barbarian tribes, would also contribute to the stock-in-trade of any leader in western Europe in those times. All these factors will be taken into account in the attempt to explain the reaction of leaders, including Arthur, to known events in Britain and Gaul.

Throughout this examination of the historical framework of late fifth- and early sixth-century Britain and Gaul, the assumption will be made that the main characters were intelligent men, even if, in some cases, their antecedents were barbarian and crude. It will therefore be assumed that any man who achieved leadership stature in those days would have behaved as intelligently and rationally in planning his affairs as we would attempt to do in modern times. There is no evidence for any change in basic human mental ability over the last few millennia, nor in particular from the year 500 to the present day. In pragmatic matters the men of those times were our equals, although they may have been more credulous in some areas. They may not have had much assistance in decision-making from documented history but this deficiency was counterbalanced by the knowledge of earlier times passed down verbally from their predecessors.

In the search for events and leaders there are, in Britain, four main historical sources for the years around 500: the books written by Gildas and Nennius, the *Annales Cambriae* and *The Anglo-Saxon Chronicle*. The authors of these may have lacked the analytic methods available to modern historians but the four sources certainly provide a framework of dates and events reasonably close to their own times.

Gildas was probably anxious to include historical information, acceptable as true by his readers, in order to justify the moral judgements he made arising from such information. Nennius simply collected all the data he could and left readers to select what they wanted.

Genealogies may be suspect in the *Chronicle* and information on defeats may have been excluded, but there can be no reason for the manipulation of dates in the earliest records. In *The Anglo-Saxon Chronicle* in particular, there is an attempt to give a record of military activities, complete with battle sites and dates, for the whole sequence of the Anglo-Saxon conquest of Britain. There may well be some uncertainty in accepting precise *Chronicle* dates, but these misgivings may be compensated for to some extent if the dates can be shown to be in reasonable agreement with information from other sources and if the battle sites can be associated with credible geographic locations.

On the other side of the Channel, Roman historians still provided information of value as late as the fifth century. For the period corresponding to the final overthrow of Roman influence in northern and southern Gaul, Gregory of Tours in his *History of the Franks* is a most useful source.

If the critical part played by any leaders in late fifth- and early sixth-century Britain and Gaul can be established by events in the invasion sequence or by divergence in the subsequent development of England and France, then as a consequence confidence in the historical and semi-historical documents relating to their careers would be greatly improved. In particular, if such a critical role can be associated with Arthur, the aim will then be to use these documents to construct a series of most probable Arthurian events which fit a time sequence and a geographical location which are consistent. The events must also support, and certainly not contradict, the accepted history of the times, even though the latter is deficient in detail.

As a preliminary to the investigation of differences in the invasion sequence north and south of the Channel and to the search for divergent developments, it is important, as explained earlier, to examine the influence that past history may have had on the behaviour of individual leaders. The next two chapters will therefore concentrate on the more general Celtic and Roman influences which must have played a considerable part in developing the abilities of military leaders, and of Arthur in particular, around the year 500. In addition to general influences, the actual history of events in the fifth century must have set limits to the possible actions of individuals in the later years of the same century. These events are outlined in Chapter 4.

Chapters 5 and 6 then deal with a detailed survey of the barbarian invasions of Gaul and Britain. The aim will be to find differences in the two sequences which may be associated with the actions of the men leading the attack and the defence in both former dioceses of the western Roman Empire. The second objective in these two chapters is to look for divergences in the subsequent development of the two countries which became, respectively, medieval France and England in the sixth and following centuries, after the invasions had ended. The divergence between the developments, if found, will direct the investigation towards discovering the causes for the difference. In particular, it will be important to discover what parts Arthur and Clovis played in causing any such divergence between the subsequent development of Britain into England and of Gaul into France. If Arthur can be shown to have played a major role, then his importance as a real historical character, equal in rank to Clovis, will have been established.

If his importance can be shown in this way, it will most certainly in large part have been due to his military capabilities, and an attempt will be made to analyse both his strategy and his tactics in the penultimate two chapters. In the first of these, the structure of Arthur's Badon campaign will be analysed. This campaign forms only the first part of one phase of the overall Anglo-Saxon invasion sequence, albeit perhaps the most important. In a later part of the same phase, the probable development of a second Arthurian campaign in East Anglia will be examined. The possible links will be explored between this second campaign, the collapse of Romano-Celtic Britain and the development of Anglo-Saxon England.

The aim is to construct a logical sequence which will take into account all the available information sources from past and present. These will include the four texts, archaeological evidence and the Celtic and Roman influences on behaviour patterns which men in those days must have felt. Account will also be taken of the results of modern research, particularly that of Professor Alcock, Dr Morris and Mr S. E. Rigold.

If the separate pieces of information can be integrated into a network of interrelated facts, all consistent one with another, then the structure as a whole becomes self-supporting and the probability of all the individual elements being correct is thereby enhanced. Particular stress will be laid on ensuring that the sequence fits the few historical dates which are known with reasonable certainty.

In the final chapter an attempt is made to outline Arthur's legacy to the history of this island and the world.

# CHAPTER 2

## The Celtic Influence

AS MENTIONED before, it is very probable that Arthur was of mixed Roman and Celtic descent; in any case, it is certain that any British leader in the initial stages of the Anglo-Saxon invasion in the fifth century would be influenced by both Roman and Celtic traditions. Although the Roman influence in Gaul at that time was stronger than in Britain (northern Gaul passed into the control of Aegidius, a high-ranking Roman soldier, in the middle years of the fifth century), the Celtic influence in both countries was still substantial. The Romans had been in Britain and Gaul for four centuries, intermarriage had certainly occurred between the higher echelons of both groups, but the Celtic way of life had by no means been eradicated. Indeed, after the Roman withdrawal from Britain in the early fifth century, Celtic customs were progressively being re-established there. Consequently, when considering the actions of any fifth-century leader in Britain or Gaul, it is essential to take account of both backgrounds. The Celtic background will be explored first.

Before the Roman conquests of Gaul and Britain, both countries had been settled by peoples of a remarkable race, the Celts. They were first identified in archaeological discoveries near the village of Halstatt in Austria. These early Celts spread westwards between 700 and 500 BC and were found to have reached a site named La Tène on Lake Neuchâtel in Switzerland by the fifth century BC. Here investigations showed that a difference had occurred in Celtic burial rites. In earlier years the leaders of the tribe were buried in wagons – that is to say, in agricultural artefacts – but when the Celts reached the La Tène site this changed. High-ranking Celts were, at the later time, buried in war chariots, indicating perhaps a more aggressive attitude. In the event, the La Tène Celts used their military capabilities to spread inexorably across Europe and beyond. Their westward expansion resulted in penetration into Gaul, their first major homeland. They subsequently moved into Britain, Ireland and north and central Spain. In Italy in 389 BC the Celtic leader Brennus defeated the Romans at the battle of the River Allia, where he outmanoeuvred the Roman general Quintus Sulpicius. He went on to sack and burn Rome and to besiege the Capitol, but withdrew while the defenders were still holding out; he was less interested in occupation than in simple looting and was bought off by the humiliated Romans. Almost 100 years later another army of Celtic tribes from Gaul moved eastwards into Greece, Macedonia and Thrace. In 270 BC some even crossed the Hellespont into Anatolia, where they settled in territory which from then on was called Galatia, after the homeland of the tribe.

The expansion to the east marked the high tide of Celtic advance and the ebb flow started in this, the third, century BC. The Celts were defeated in Macedonia by Antigonus Gonatus and, a little later, they lost their foothold in Asia when the Galatians were defeated by Attalus of Pergamon in 241 BC. In Italy the expansion of Rome had resulted in the annexation in 283 BC of the Ager Gallicus, the Adriatic coastal district south of the River Po held by the Gauls. This dispossession rankled and some 60 years later a Gallic army moved south against Rome. After initial success at Clusium, they were returning north with their plunder when they were caught between two Roman armies at Telamon in 225 BC and almost totally destroyed. At about the same time, the Celts in Spain came under pressure from the growing power of Carthage and in the second century BC the Celts in Gaul felt the impact of the Cimbri attacking from Jutland.

It was, however, the increasing power of Rome in the first century BC which saw the end of Celtic independence in most of western Europe. By the year 100 BC Roman provinces had been created along nearly all of the northern shore of the Mediterranean and, with the defeat of Carthage, a foothold in northern Africa had been gained. In particular, eastern Spain and southern Gaul were by now part of the Roman state, whose campaign against the Celts continued. This campaign gained momentum with the advent of a Roman commander of exceptional military abilities: Gaius Julius Caesar. He had developed his skills in the art of war while serving as a provincial governor in Spain and he returned to Rome to be elected consul in 59 BC. As consul, he was allocated two provinces, Cisalpine Gaul and Illyricum, but by his good fortune the governor of Transalpine Gaul died and Caesar managed to bring this new province also under his authority. He knew that Transalpine Gaul, or Gallia Narbonensis, was a splendid platform for launching a campaign against Celtic north-western Europe and he was right. Within a period of seven years, from 59 to 52 BC, Caesar had completely subjugated Gaul and had found the time to cross the Channel twice to campaign in Britain. It is from these campaigns that the best information relating to the strengths and weaknesses of the Celts can be assessed. These attributes are important for understanding their possible influence on Romano-Celtic leaders in future times.

The fact that the Celts were certainly brave and fearless fighters can be deduced from the achievement of the broad expansion from Gaul to Galatia in the fifth and fourth centuries BC. Nevertheless, a more detailed description of their prowess, and of their progressive decline, which reached its final stages when the western Celts were faced with the growing power of republican Rome, is provided by Caesar's commentaries on his own campaigns. Two Celtic commanders attained fame in these wars, one in Gaul and one in Britain. Although both were defeated in the end by Caesar, they had some success which not only reflected favourably on their own abilities but also demonstrated the courage and skills of the Celtic warriors. The British campaigns will be considered first.

Almost in the middle of his campaign against the north-western Celts in Gaul, Caesar decided to move against Britain. The landing took place in 55 BC towards the end of summer, rather late in the season for a military campaign, and it is possible that he intended to use this first British campaign as a means of gaining experience for a main assault at a later date. The force he used was relatively small, comprising only two legions plus some native auxiliaries. He planned to include cavalry but the main cavalry transports were delayed by unfavourable tides and the landing went ahead without cavalry support. The two legions were put ashore near Deal and, after some initial difficulties, formed up on the beach. Once in position, they charged the less organized British and quickly put them to flight. The absence of cavalry made it difficult to follow up this advantage and, what was worse, a double crisis developed shortly after the landing. The cavalry transports, having finally set off for Britain, were hit by a severe storm and scattered. The same storm damaged many of the ships lying off Deal. Increased activity by the British and a surprise attack on the Seventh Legion were countered by Caesar, but his position was not secure. He withdrew from Britain before the winter, probably intending to return in the following year.

He did return one year later and this time deployed five legions and a large force of cavalry in a much more substantial expedition across the Channel. On the other hand, the British had also benefited from the experience gained a year earlier. In order to obtain the advantage of a unified military command, they had appointed Cassivellaunus, the king of a tribe (possibly the Catuvellauni) living just north of the Thames, to be commander-in-chief of the British forces.

In his earliest engagements Cassivellaunus showed considerable skill in opposing Caesar by using mobile tactics in place of a static pitched battle. The British used both cavalry and chariots in their mobile approach and Caesar had not encountered the latter in his earlier campaigns in Gaul. The chariots, pulled by two ponies, carried both a driver and a fighting man. The latter used the chariot either as a mobile platform for launching javelins or as a means of transport to a place where he could dismount and take advantage of increased stability for throwing his javelins. Although they could deal with the chariots, the Roman cavalry in the early engagements found that if they advanced too far ahead of the infantry legions, javelins from the dismounted chariot infantry could cause them serious problems. As a consequence, the first clashes between Romans and British were inconclusive.

A new tactical response was needed and Caesar quickly realized that the answer was closer association, both physical and by chain of command, between cavalry and the infantry legions. This new tactic resulted in a pitched battle in which the British forces were defeated.

These early encounters between Romans and Celts underlined basic differences in their approaches to battle. The Celts were fearless and emotional fighters, favouring an initial somewhat disordered charge, hopefully to persuade the enemy to break ranks and flee. The Roman tactics were different. In attack or defence their actions were essentially well ordered, with units as far as possible always under the direction of the general commanding. In most cases the Roman tactic succeeded.

Even after his first decisive defeat, Cassivellaunus remained on the attack. He decided to use guerrilla tactics and to avoid pitched battle, making full use of his mobile forces. He deployed some 4,000 charioteers to harass the Roman forces, with useful results. Nevertheless, he was defeated in the end and this was due in part to another Celtic characteristic.

The Celtic peoples always had a strong feeling for the importance of their own tribe; they were less concerned with racial loyalty. In practical terms, this meant that, in spite of the agreement to make

Cassivellaunus supreme commander of the British forces, the Trinovantes, tribal enemies of Cassivellaunus, felt no self-reproach in sending supplies to Caesar and, in return, asking for help against their tribal enemy. As an additional bonus, they revealed the site of Cassivellaunus's base near Wheathampstead, which, of course, Caesar attacked and destroyed.

Even after this setback Cassivellaunus did not concede victory; he instructed his allies in Kent to attack the Roman naval base. They were unsuccessful and the British finally gave in. Owing to unrest in Gaul, Caesar could not follow up his victory and, after claiming tribute and agreeing reasonable terms, the Romans returned to Gaul. The Roman conquest of most of the island had to wait 90 years for the Emperor Claudius to initiate a new campaign in AD 43 which finally resulted in complete Roman control south of Hadrian's Wall.

Before his expedition to Britain, Caesar had already undertaken several campaigns in Gaul, chiefly in the eastern part of the country, attacking and defeating the Helvetii and the Nervii tribes. By the year 57 BC he certainly felt that peace had been brought to the whole of Gaul, until the rebellion of the Venetii in the north-west showed his error. The suppression of the Venetii took most of the next year and was followed by the British expeditions described above.

The unrest which had forced Caesar to return to Gaul had been initiated by the massacre of a Roman general, Sabinus, and his legion on the Meuse by Ambiorix, the chief of the Eburones. This encouraged the Carnutes and the Senones to show active opposition to the imperial power, and they massacred the chiefs who had been placed over them by the Romans. Full-scale revolt in the rest of Gaul followed. On his return, Caesar put down the rebellion with his accustomed energy and speed of reaction.

However, as in Britain a few years earlier, the Celtic tribes had profited by the experience gained in previous campaigns and appointed Vercingetorix as commander-in-chief of all the Gallic tribes. He was the king of the Arverni, a tribe living in the Auvergne region of modern France, and an exceptionally able military leader. Even so, he faced problems very similar to those faced by Cassivellaunus in Britain, finding it difficult to develop a tactical plan which would enable his relatively disorganized forces to face the disciplined Roman legions on anything like equal terms. In addition, again like Cassivellaunus, he had to take account of the very strong possibility that some tribes would take the Roman side in opposition to his own forces. Indeed, many of the tribes on the southern and eastern frontiers of Gaul declared for Rome and there were even some in his own tribe who favoured Roman control. Those leaning towards Rome included the Narbonnaise and Allobroges tribe in the south and the Remi and Lingones around Reims and Langres. The Aedui in Burgundy wavered between support and opposition.

Vercingetorix was, however, an intelligent strategist and he decided to take advantage of Caesar's temporary absence in Italy, watching over his interests in Rome. The Gallic leader decided to attack the Roman forces in the centre and north of Gaul, while, at the same time, using a considerable part of his forces in the south-east to cut off supplies to the northern legions and to prevent reinforcements from Italy coming to their aid. He did not find it easy to execute this plan. He feared that a party in his own tribe who were not unfriendly towards Caesar might mount an attack on his rearguard if he moved any of his forces south-eastwards. The intransigence of the Aedui could also introduce the danger of a flank attack. These two problems introduced an element of indecision and this, coupled with Caesar's characteristic speed of reaction, enabled the Roman reinforcements to bypass the Arverni, link up with the northern legions and face Vercingetorix in the region of Sens. The result was a pitched battle which, without total defeat for the Gauls, certainly went in Caesar's favour. From this time forward, Vercingetorix decided to avoid pitched battles and, like Cassivellaunus, to attempt a guerrilla form of warfare. Both sides followed a scorched-earth policy.

In the course of the following campaign, which was to end in complete conquest of Gaul, Caesar laid siege to Avaricum (Bourges), the chief town of the Bituriges. After 27 days the town was taken and the inhabitants massacred; a second defeat for the Gallic forces. However, the tide was about to turn – at least for a short time.

To follow up his success at Avaricum, Caesar resolved to attack Vercingetorix's own tribe. He invaded the heart of the Auvergne and laid siege to Gergovia, the stronghold of the Arverni. In order to meet this challenge, Vercingetorix had not followed the usual plan of placing all his forces inside the fortress and defending it entirely from within. He had divided his forces, retaining only part inside. He then took an unconventional course by occupying an adjacent hill with the rest of his troops, putting himself in the tactical position of being able to attack Caesar's legions investing the stronghold from both front and rear. Caesar was forced to retreat from this untenable situation with the loss of almost 1,000 men.

This was the first major success for the Gallic army and it had the beneficial result of convincing the Aedui that Vercingetorix might well win the war. In consequence, they joined the rebellion and several other tribes followed suit. Caesar, fearing that his line of communications with Italy might be cut, decided to retreat from the north and regroup in the south. He reached Transalpine Gaul before halting to reinforce and to await the opportunity for a new initiative.

Vercingetorix was impatient and, feeling that victory was within his grasp, he abandoned his decision never again to fight a pitched battle and decided to attack Caesar. It was an unwise choice. He was defeated and fell back under pursuit to the fortress of Alesia on Mont Auxois, near Dijon. Caesar was still smarting after his failure at Gergovia and was quite determined that the siege of Alesia would have a very different outcome. This time Vercingetorix did not have either the time or the strength to repeat the Gergovia plan and all his forces, about equal in number to those of Caesar, withdrew inside the fortress. Caesar immediately ringed the fortress with his own troops, but he knew that this disposition carried with it serious disadvantages. First, the size of the ring meant that the Roman legions would be spread very thinly round the whole circumference. In addition, it was very probable that Vercingetorix would call for assistance from the other Gallic tribes and, when they arrived, Caesar could be attacked from front and rear, as he had been at Gergovia.

The plans that Caesar made to counter these disadvantages involved using the comprehensive range of siege tactics that the Roman army had at its command. He surrounded the fortress with several rings of defences. The first and inner ring was a *contravallum*, a ditch six metres (20 feet) wide with perpendicular sides, intended to slow down or stop any attack coming from inside the fortress. Some 400 paces further out, a second ring of defences was constructed consisting of two ditches, the inner filled with water, with a palisade and rampart behind them. Anticipating an attack from relieving forces, Caesar then constructed a third ring of defences facing outwards. With all this in place, the Romans waited for the attack, which came, as expected, from both inside and outside the fortress.

Vercingetorix's appeal for help brought a Gallic army at least twice the size of the Roman forces to support the defenders, so placing Caesar at a disadvantage of about three to one. In spite of the numerical inequality, the defenders were unable to break out. In the battle which then followed, the Gallic army attacking from the outside was also defeated. Vercingetorix had no other course of action but to surrender and, although there was still some spirited opposition in the north, the revolt finally crumbled and all Gaul became part of the Roman empire.

Gaul fell in 50 BC, but in Britain there was a respite from Roman aggression for some 90 years. During this time Cassivellaunus, following his partial success in opposing the Romans, became preeminent in the south of Britain. One of his successors, Cunobelinus (Shakespeare's Cymbeline), ruled both the Catuvellauni and the Trinovantes and moved his capital to Camulodunum (Colchester). After his death, around the year AD 41, he was succeeded by his two sons, Togodumnus and Caratacus, who continued the expansionist policies of their predecessors, attacking the Dobunni in the west and the Atrebates in the south-west. Clearly the energy and aggressive attributes of the British Celts had not in any way been diminished by their early encounters with Caesar. A second Roman invasion was, however, imminent.

At about this time Britain had become the safe haven for the Gallic Druids, the religious leaders of the Celts throughout the west. In Gaul the Druids were strongly anti-Roman and were consequently persecuted by the Roman authorities. The existence of the Druid haven in Britain and a desire to finish the task started by Julius Caesar were probably factors in persuading the Emperor Claudius to plan a second invasion of Britain.

The expedition was placed under the command of Aulus Plautius, who landed at Richborough in AD 43 and was opposed somewhat tardily by the brothers Togodumnus and Caratacus. After some skirmishes, the British withdrew to the Medway. Once again the Celts failed to present a united front against the greater enemy and the Dobunni approached Plautius with an offer of peace, which was accepted. Plautius then advanced to the Medway and fought a decisive battle near Rochester which led to a further retreat of the British across the Thames and into Essex. At some time within this period Togodumnus was killed, leaving Caratacus in sole command.

This change in leadership may possibly have stiffened British resistance, but the matter was not put to the test, since Plautius halted his advance in order to await Claudius's arrival from Rome to put the imperial seal on the conquest. There is some uncertainty as to the exact role played by the emperor when he arrived. It is possible that some further military engagements were led by Claudius personally, but he soon entered Camulodunum as victor, although Caratacus escaped capture and fled to the west of the island. Camulodunum became the first capital of the Roman administration in Britain and Aulus Plautius the first governor.

The Claudian invasion of southern Britain corresponded with Caesar's first campaign in Gaul some 100 years earlier in that Roman conquest spread from the south-east northwards and westwards. However, the first four years of Plautius's governorship was a period when the Romans consolidated their gains; it was when he was succeeded by the second governor, Ostorius Scapula, that hostilities began afresh. After an absence of about five years, Caratacus reappeared as the leader of the Silures in south Wales. He later became commander of all the British forces of revolt, working from a base in the territory of the Ordovices in central Wales. In this he was the able successor of Cassivellaunus and played the same role as Vercingetorix 100 years earlier in Gaul. He had, however, little success.

He faced Ostorius on a river site, probably the Severn, but although he had the advantage of position, he was unable to match the discipline and organized superiority of the Romans. He was defeated and fled to the Brigantes in the north. With typical lack of intertribal loyalty, the queen of the Brigantes, Cartimandua, handed him over to the Romans. In contrast to the treatment meted out to the defeated Vercingetorix, who was executed by Caesar, Caratacus was taken to Rome, where he so impressed Claudius that both he and his family were pardoned. The defeat of Caratacus did not, however, mark the end of the revolt. Ostorius faced further trouble from the Silures, who were persuading other tribes to join the rebellion. These problems were all too much for the governor, who died from what we would perhaps now say was a stress-related illness.

The two governors who followed Ostorius both faced a Britain which remained turbulent. The first, Didius Gallus, encountered further trouble, this time from the Brigantes, where Venutius, the husband of Cartimandua, had taken an anti-Roman stance in opposition to his wife. Didius sent north troops who settled the matter in favour of Cartimandua. After the Emperor Claudius died, his successor, Nero, replaced Didius by another distinguished soldier, Quintus Veranius, who died shortly after his appointment.

It was under the next governor, Suetonius Paulinus, that the most memorable revolt developed. Paulinus was a very ambitious soldier and, after two years in the field, he was completing a successful campaign in north Wales in the year AD 60. On the island of Anglesey he had defeated a British force, probably Ordovices strongly supported by Druids. The island was a very important Druid centre, perhaps the most important in western Europe, and Paulinus's victory finally broke the power of the Druids in both Britain and Gaul. During this campaign, however, even more serious trouble was brewing in eastern Britain.

As a successful soldier, Paulinus may have delegated too much authority to the head of the civil department of his governor's office. Both before and during the Anglesey campaign, the procurator, Decianus Catus, and his local officers were treating the Iceni in eastern Britain particularly badly. Their king, Prasutagus, had just died and, as was customary for a client king in the Roman Empire, he left the kingdom to his two daughters with the emperor as co-heir. By custom, this legal arrangement usually meant that the emperor took over part of the kingdom as an imperial estate and the local heir was left to govern the major part as before, acting as client ruler. Catus and his officers proceeded, however, to take over the whole kingdom, and when the late king's wife, Boudicca, protested, she was flogged and her daughters raped.

The result was an immediate conflagration and Colchester, almost unprotected by any military forces, fell to Boudicca after a resistance of only two days. London was the next target of the British forces, chiefly Iceni and Trinovantes, and part of the Ninth Legion was almost destroyed in an unsuccessful attempt to stem the advance. London was pillaged and Boudicca then turned north to attack and destroy Verulamium (St Albans). According to Tacitus, some 70,000 died in the attacks on Colchester, London and St Albans. Meanwhile, Paulinus, hearing of the disasters, brought his forces post-haste back from north Wales, about 10,000 men in all, including the Fourteenth Legion and part of the Twentieth, together with some supporting auxiliaries and cavalry.

By this time Boudicca's force was much larger than the Roman's, probably about 50,000 fighting men, and it was moving north to meet the smaller Roman army moving south. The two armies met somewhere in the Midlands, at a site carefully chosen by Paulinus. He placed his troops at the head of a slope leading up a narrow valley; his rear was protected by a dense forest and his flanks by the sides of the valley. The British gathered at the foot of the slope with their wagons behind them, to be used by the women and children camp-followers as a grandstand from which to view the battle. The usual undisciplined Celtic charge up the slope was met by a hail of javelins. Several attacks were probably repelled in this way until the Roman command to advance was given. The following disciplined countercharge by the legions in wedge formation pinned the British against the wagons, where they were slaughtered. A figure of 80,000 British dead against 400 Roman was quoted by Tacitus, but the British count was almost certainly exaggerated.

Boudicca escaped but died shortly afterwards. Paulinus exacted a violent revenge on all the tribes who had supported the revolt and in the end Britain, like Gaul, became a province in the Roman Empire. Celtic independence was extinguished in the whole of western Europe apart from Ireland and some areas in Scotland.

The history of Celtic defeat at the hands of the Romans followed similar courses in Gaul and Britain although separated in time by more than a century. The military abilities of the Gallic and British Celts were also very similar – great personal bravery and *élan* but little discipline and organization. The campaigns of Caesar in Gaul and of Claudius and Paulinus in Britain clearly showed the consequences of the two Celtic military attributes of indiscipline and disorganization which contributed to final defeat in both countries. Another cause of the defeat was the frequent failure of Celtic intertribal loyalty in both countries. On many occasions, although a supreme commander of the combined Celtic tribes had been agreed, some tribes defected to the Roman side and seriously weakened their compatriots. This particular characteristic may explain the absence of any large unified Celtic state in Europe even at the height of Celtic expansion.

Some Celtic lack of discipline and lack of military organization may well have persisted into Arthurian times, but by then the Romano-Celtic attitudes would very likely have been tempered through many years of experience of the Roman contrast. The failure of intertribal loyalty can, however, still be detected in those later times and will be shown to have had substantial historical consequences.

There were other Celtic characteristics which helped to shape history and which also might well have affected the actions of fifth-century leaders (see Markale 1976: Chapter 7). These arose from the peculiarly Celtic social structure, which differed in some vital respects from the corresponding Roman form, and their consequences can therefore best be assessed by examining the contrast between the two systems. Like the Romans, the Celts were divided by a three-tier social structure: in the top rank were the king and the priests, in the second rank the warriors and in the third the ordinary people. Beyond this similarity in the overall division, there were nevertheless important differences.

For the Romans in the early days the first rank certainly included the king and the priests, but this changed when Rome became a republic. The king was replaced first by the consuls and then by the emperor. In the days of the empire, which coincided with growth of secular power, the priests, although remaining in the first rank, became less important. At the same time, in order to emphasize the power of the emperor, one of the priestly titles, Pontifex Maximus, was taken over as an imperial title. In the second rank of Roman society were the patricians, a class which included the Senate, rich land-owners, the leading families and the knights or equestrians. In the third rank were the plebeians or ordinary citizens.

The main differences between the Celtic and the Roman three-tiered social structures lay in the two topmost tiers. Although the first rank in both cases contained the secular and the religious powers, the relation between these two powers was quite different for the Celts. The secular power, in the person of the emperor, became totally dominant in Rome but this was not so in Celtic Britain or Gaul. In their system the king had little power but great symbolic significance. He had to be present in battle, for example, and to speak before any of his people in tribal discussions. On the other hand, the religious leader, the Druid, could speak first, even before the king, and it was his duty to interpret the law and act as judge. The Celtic second rank was also different from the Roman in that it included the masters of arts and crafts, classes which in Rome were in the third rank or even lower as slaves. The limitations of regal power, the exceptional authority of the Druids and the importance given to poets and craftsmen in the second tier all contributed to the power of the tribal assembly and diminished the control of the executive leader of the tribe.

This weakness to some extent explains the problems faced by Cassivellaunus, Vercingetorix, Caratacus and Boudicca. Each of these leaders was given authority to lead confederations of tribes against the Roman aggressor and each must have had some experience of Roman military tactics. Nevertheless, the Celtic method of taking decisions in assembly diminished the ability of the leader to take action based on his own judgement; just as in the more local tribal assembly the king was constrained by the attitude of his warriors and by the Druid adviser. Campaigns were made more difficult to organize due to these limitations forced on the commander-in-chief. In contrast, in the Roman system, at a time of national crisis a dictator was appointed for a period of six months with absolute power to take any decision he felt necessary. Success followed more easily from this unified command structure.

In spite of the fact that the Arthurian legend is not the main concern here, it is interesting to note that the relation between King Arthur and his knights as portrayed in the story cycle has stronger links with the Celtic concept of kingship than with the medieval concept prevalent at the time the stories were written. Arthur is first among equals, sitting at a round table where precedence has been eliminated. In most of the stories Arthur maintains the traditions of the court as a symbolic head, while the knights go forth as individuals and are the real heroes of the tales. This aspect of Arthur's kingship is most likely derived from traditions passed down to the medieval writers either in the bardic poems or in stories passed down by word of mouth. It indicates that the Celtic tradition of kingship had largely replaced Roman by the end of the fifth century in Britain. It also shows that appreciation of the Celtic tradition had been passed down in story form to medieval times, where it appeared in sharp contrast to the decisive power exercised by medieval kings.

Finally, one other social characteristic of the Celts should be included, although its effect in later centuries was greater in Britain than in Gaul: their language. The speech of the Celts not only set them apart from their Roman conquerors but also in Britain formed a basis for a culture which has survived to the present day. The Welsh language has outlasted both the Roman and Anglo-Saxon invasions of the island.

The language spoken by the Celts at the time of the Roman conquest is not known with certainty but two branches, apart from the Celtiberian spoken in Spain, can be traced forward to the present day. The first branch, Brythonic, developed into the Welsh, Cornish and Breton variants, and the second, Goidelic, into the Irish, Scottish Gaelic and Manx. The Celtic tongue spoken in Gaul has no direct descendant today but is thought to have been closely related to Brythonic. It is difficult to be certain, but it is possible that use of the Celtic languages declined more rapidly in Gaul than in Britain due to the former's greater proximity to Rome. Revival of Celtic languages certainly occurred in Britain in the fifth century and may have stimulated the regrowth of Celtic traditions, but a similar revival did not happen in Gaul.

Celtic traditions and customs were initially overlaid to some degree by the weight of the Roman military and civil organization during the centuries which followed the conquest of Britain and Gaul, but they were not lost, and in the fifth century, when Roman power receded from western Europe, the Celtic way of life reappeared to influence the peoples and their leaders. Among the Celtic influences which were to reappear and be of particular concern in Arthurian times were the limitation of the powers of the king, the continued preference for unorganized combat and the lack of racial loyalty. It will become clear later that all these factors influenced Arthur in the late fifth and early sixth centuries.

This reappearance and growth of Celtic influences did not, however, exclude the retention of some Roman concepts and traditions, which persisted into the fifth century. As a result, both Roman and Celtic influences existed side by side to guide western leaders in their opposition to the invasions from the Germanic lands in the fifth and sixth centuries.

# The Roman Influence

IN THE previous chapter attention was concentrated on those Celtic influences which may well have been felt by leaders in later centuries. At the same time, due to the close interaction between the Celtic and Roman civilizations, it was impossible to exclude some Roman influences experienced by the Celts in their many military engagements with Rome before and during the progress of the Roman conquest, and which persisted throughout the period of Roman rule. In this chapter attention will be directed specifically towards the Roman influences which developed after the Celts had been brought within the Roman Empire.

The military victories over Vercingetorix in Gaul and Boudicca in Britain began a gradual Romanization of Celtic society and a progressive integration of both countries into the rest of the Roman Empire. This process provided the second background influence which must have been felt by the late fifth- and early sixth-century leaders in Britain and Gaul. One of the first consequences of the Roman success was a modification of the social structure. The ruling authority was now the Roman emperor, whose power was exercised through the military strength of the legions, which also provided support for the civil administration, whose prime function was the collection of taxes.

At first, client kingdoms were allowed, with king and assembly retaining some control. The same tolerance was not extended to the power of the Druids. Their authority had been decisively eliminated, first in Gaul and then in Britain by the victory of Paulinus on Anglesey just before the revolt led by Boudicca. However, as in Gaul, the British institutions of king and assembly were, after the succession of Roman victories, quickly superseded by Roman counterparts based on the authority of Roman governors, supported by the legions located at forts such as Colchester, Lincoln, Chester and Caerleon.

After the elimination of the first rank of the Celtic social structure, the second rank, the Celtic nobility and warriors, retained a measure of control through the development of provincial councils. Although their main function was to show loyalty to Rome, they could, by failing to express thanks to a retiring governor, inspire an imperial investigation. Such a possibility exercised considerable restraint on the unbridled tyranny of any governor. In both Britain and Gaul after their conquest, the second rank of Celtic society accepted the authority of Rome and the two integrated to some extent to form Romano-Celtic institutions, similar to the patrician institutions that existed in Rome, in which land ownership played a major role.

As in Italy, then in Gaul and finally in Britain, the estates of the wealthy gradually spread across the countryside. At the centre of these estates was the Roman villa, a country house which, in many cases, displayed great opulence and sophistication. The network of villas spread across Gaul and southern Britain and reached a peak at the end of the third century. Some of the early villas were small timbered buildings, although stone structures soon followed and these reached considerable size: the villa at Fishbourne in Sussex and several in Gaul, such as the one at Chiragan, could match the palaces in Rome and Italy. Small hamlets or villages were also to be found in the countryside, some of which existed alongside the villas. In later times villages developed on or around villas that had been abandoned or destroyed. Towns were needed as administration centres for tax gathering and as market centres both for food and for the interchange of the products of the art and craft industries of the empire. These towns were small by our standards, ranging in size usually between ten and 100 hectares (25 and 250 acres). Within the towns standard Roman buildings started to appear, such as the forum, temples and public baths. Both villas and towns needed the protection afforded by the Roman army, based in forts often placed near towns or in strategic positions to control communications. In the latter case, the presence of a fort would probably encourage the development of a town nearby.

All these developments took time to materialize, but by the end of the first century considerable progress had been made in urban development. Due to the earlier conquest, progress was faster in Gaul than in Britain. Nevertheless, London had become the provincial capital and a substantial building programme was under way there. The basilica and forum had been started in the Flavian period and administrative buildings were being added. The architectural style of these was very different from that of the Celtic structures which existed prior to the conquest.

Research to date has shown that the architectural expertise of the Celts did not quite keep pace with their high-class craftwork in armour, weapons and personal adornments. In the first century BC some Celts lived in the sort of village which was discovered by Arthur Bulleid in 1892 near Glastonbury. Some 90 huts were excavated on the site, each having a circular plan and being constructed of vertical timbers joined by hurdles, with clay floors and a central hearth. Other structures have been found within the boundaries of Iron Age hill-forts and some of these show evidence of rectangular buildings set in straight lines to form streets, following the pattern set by Roman fortified camps. Some stone huts have been discovered, chiefly in the north, and perhaps the most advanced stone structures were the brochs of northern Scotland, round stone towers about 13 metres (42 feet) high.

In neither Britain nor Gaul was the Celtic background entirely lost, but in both countries the Roman infrastructure of villas, towns and forts was adopted and grew steadily, to reach a peak in the third and fourth centuries, before declining in parallel with the decline of empire. By the later years of the fifth century in Britain, most of the Roman villas and town buildings had either been abandoned or been destroyed and this was also true of many parts of Gaul. Consequently Roman civil architecture had little influence on leadership or people in the two countries after Roman withdrawal.

There were, however, other Roman structures which were abandoned but not easily destroyed. These were the roads which were built as part of the military process of empire-building in Britain and in Gaul. As the Roman army advanced into non-Roman territory, a road was built as a tactical necessity to facilitate supply and communications, to bring up reserves and replacements, and, when Roman power was established, to assist civil administration and trade. The main road system in Gaul spread from Marseilles north to Lyons and Châlons, from which cities roads stretched westwards to Armorica (Brittany), northwards to Boulogne, and eastwards to the Rhine and Danube. In Britain the road system led from Kent to London, and from there roads fanned out, tracing the advance of the legions east to Colchester, north to Lincoln, north-west to Wroxeter and west to Silchester and the West Country. There was one very important road, the Fosse Way, leading north-east from Ilchester to Lincoln and linking all the roads radiating north and west from London. Although the road system went into disrepair once the Roman Empire declined in the west, the roads themselves would almost certainly have been usable during the fifth and sixth centuries and must have had some considerable military significance over that period.

In the fields of law and civil administration, the Romans imposed their own very successful pragmatic methods. These were most efficient in exploiting the gains made during the military conquests, and the Romano-British and Gallo-Roman societies were constrained to adopt and use Roman methods in these crucial areas of human activity. In Britain the Roman law and administration methods may have partially survived the collapse of Roman power in the early years of the fifth century, but they certainly did not survive the Anglo-Saxon invasions which reached final success late in the sixth century. As will be seen later, this was not the case in Gaul.

The Romans were more tolerant in matters of religion after they had suppressed the Druids, whose authority in Celtic society was unacceptable to the imperial power. In the early centuries they demanded acknowledgement of the divinity of their emperors, but after that they were content to permit worship of local deities. Celtic gods and goddesses were worshipped in both Britain and Gaul equally with those of Rome. When the Druids were displaced from their positions of power, they were replaced first by priests of the Romano-Celtic pantheon and then by bishops and priests following the spread of Christianity throughout the Roman world. In this sphere at least the Roman influence, exercised by the Pope, endured well into the Middle Ages.

As a matter of practicality, the Roman army, and the administrators who followed, brought their language with them and it became necessary for the subject peoples to develop a working knowledge of the Roman tongue. Latin as the language of the army, the administration and trade became dominant in the towns, while native Celtic was probably more in use in the British countryside and also, at least in the early years after the conquest, in the countryside in Gaul. In both countries Latin flourished as the written language well into medieval times.

In one field above all others Roman influence was unquestionably crucial: the military sphere (see Webster 1981). The Celtic tribes in the west were subdued by the Romans with their superior military tactics and high-quality generalship. Even brave and courageous fighters led by skilled and intelligent leaders such as Cassivellaunus or Vercingetorix could not match the disciplined Roman legions led by men such as Caesar. Up to the end of the fourth century, there is no doubt that the fighting qualities of the legions were one of the most important factors in maintaining the power and authority of the Roman Empire.

The organization of the legion was subject to change, but it was always an infantry unit about 5,000 strong. The legionary commander, the legate, was of senatorial rank and was supported by six staff officers, the tribunes, of either senatorial or equestrian rank. The legion was divided into ten cohorts, each led by a praefectus and comprising six centuries (originally 100 men but in imperial days 60), each led by a centurion. These latter officers, equivalent to the modern sergeant, were the backbone of the legion. A small force of cavalry was attached to each legion, only about 300 strong and reflecting the lower status of the cavalry with respect to the infantry.

Some idea of the tactics used by the legion in battle can be gained from descriptions of engagements and campaigns described by early historians. Pre-eminent among these is Julius Caesar in his account of his own actions against the Celts. A noteworthy textbook of military tactics entitled *The Art of War* was written by one Julius Frontinus, a governor of Britain from AD 74 to 78, in which he claimed to provide the only systematic study of the subject. Unfortunately, a fragment of his text is all that survives, but a fourth-century writer, Vegetius, in his *Epitoma Rei Militaris* (*Summary of Military Matters*) probably incorporated much of Frontinus on tactics.

Vegetius lays down the conditions which must be met before battle is joined, dealing with such matters as the choice of terrain, preferring, for example, that Roman troops should be placed on higher ground than the enemy, and that the wind should if possible blow in the face of the enemy. Each soldier should be given a space of about a metre on either side with two behind to the next rank. Normally the legions would hold the centre, with the cavalry on the wings; in this position the latter could prevent any outflanking of the centre. If and when the legions gained the ascendancy, the cavalry could move forward and cut down the enemy in retreat. One exceptionally useful tactic employed by the legion was described as the 'wedge'. At the right moment, when the enemy was most disorganized, small groups of the legion in wedge formation would advance into the enemy ranks to engage in close combat. Here the short Roman sword (*gladius*) could be used for thrusting rather than slashing and would have a decisive advantage over the Celtic long sword. (The *gladius* had a double edge and could also be used for cutting as well as thrusting.) The battle plans of Suetonius Paulinus in his final defeat of Boudicca, as outlined in Chapter 2, provide a perfect textbook illustration of these Roman legionary tactics.

Although in these early centuries of the Roman Empire the legions were almost always successful, there were instances when they were defeated, usually due to inferior leadership. The most decisive defeats are those which are best remembered and one such was the defeat of Quinctilius Varus, which terminated Augustus's dream of ever placing the Roman frontier on the Elbe.

The province of Germania, on the west bank of the Rhine, had been finally established through the efforts of Ahenobarbus and Vinicius around the year AD 4 and an experienced administrator, Varus, had been appointed governor to complete pacification and, hopefully, to extend the empire eastwards. Unfortunately, he lacked military ability. In AD 9 he led three legions eastwards from his base towards the Elbe. He had reached about the half-way point and was crossing the wild country of the Teutoburger Forest when he was ambushed by a German force led by Arminius. This German prince of the Cherusci tribe had served in the Roman armies and possibly knew more of Roman tactics than did Varus. In the first encounter the terrain favoured the Germans and, although the Romans held firm, they suffered under German throwing spears without being able to come to close quarters. On the second day the cavalry was ordered to attack, but the forest was not suitable terrain for cavalry action and they were destroyed piecemeal. On the final day, without cavalry to protect the flanks, the remnants of the legions were slaughtered and Varus committed suicide. Discipline and efficient weaponry were not enough to secure victory without the tactical skill of the commander. In addition, the value of cavalry had been demonstrated, but only if used in the appropriate circumstances.

The disgrace of defeat was not, however, allowed to go unavenged and some six years later Germanicus Caesar, brother of the Emperor Claudius, led another campaign against Arminius. An indecisive action was fought in the same area and Arminius's wife was captured. In the next year Arminius was finally defeated, but the campaign had proved to be both difficult and costly and, as a consequence, any hope of placing the Roman frontier beyond the Rhine was abandoned.

In addition to the excellent weaponry, organization and tactics of the legions, the Romans also developed an advanced system of military engineering. Its simplest form was the protected legionary campsite built at the end of a day's march by the legionaries themselves. On a much larger scale, the skill of the Roman engineers was used to protect the frontiers of the empire (see Webster 1981: Chapter 2). The natural frontiers of the Rhine and the Danube were joined by the Limes Germanicus, a fortified frontier some 320 kilometres (200 miles) long. In Britain the Antonine Wall and Hadrian's Wall were built across the narrowest part of the island to keep the Picts at bay, and some of these structures have survived. Even today one can walk the length of Hadrian's Wall and examine some of the associated forts. There are also some remains of the line of forts built by the Romans on the coast of East Anglia and along the south coast. These were intended to assist in the protection of the east coast of Britain from barbarian raids by Saxons and other tribes coming from their bases in north-western Europe. The value of Roman military engineering has already been shown in the description of Caesar's defeat of Vercingetorix at Avaricum.

For attack and reduction of enemy strongholds, the Romans made use of siege engines which were superior to any available to the rest of Europe. Their battering rams and *ballista* (catapults) were mechanically quite sophisticated. The latter could throw a stone weighing 25 kilograms (45 pounds) a distance of 400 metres (434 yards) or more. The use of all these engines of war and military structures required the services of a large number of technically skilled men for both construction and maintenance. These included surveyors, architects, builders, carpenters, wheelwrights, blacksmiths, hydraulic engineers and many others, listed in a second-century work, *De Rei Militari*, by Paternus, who was also a source for Vegetius.

However, as the western Roman Empire entered its period of collapse in the fifth century and as the Dark Ages opened in Britain, the disintegration of Roman society and the lack of financial support from Rome terminated both the stationing of Roman troops in Britain and the supply of military technicians. As a consequence, the construction and maintenance of such weaponry, forts and machines tailed off in the fifth century and all that remained were the ideas which had made an impression on military minds and the larger-scale structures that were best able to withstand the ravages of time.

An interesting example of the persistence of the memory of past military technology is provided by the archaeological investigation of the South Cadbury hill-top fort which, as mentioned earlier, was undertaken by Professor Alcock in the search for Arthur's headquarters. Underneath the remains of a Saxon wall was a structure identified as the gate of the reconstructed fortifications built around the year 500. This gate, with a single tower built over it, all of timber construction, was found to be very similar to the gates of other minor Roman forts built in much earlier times. Thus, from the Arthurian period, there is archaeological evidence that, in contrast with the ruin or disappearance of Roman civilian structures, the memory of Roman military structures persisted and was, moreover, used to build military defences some 100 years after the Roman departure from Britain. This direct evidence of the use of Roman military technology by leaders of Britain at the end of the fifth century makes it just as probable that such leaders would remember Roman tactics and organization in the military field and would use them in the defence of the island. Such a probability would be even greater in Gaul, where the Roman withdrawal was delayed until the last quarter of the fifth century.

The tactics remembered, however, would not be the legionary tactics described by Vegetius but something quite different. There was no way that the Romano-Celtic societies of the fifth century could either organize or equip a military unit of some 5,000 men to resemble the Roman legion. However, the reason for remembering another facet of Roman military expertise stemmed from the second major defeat suffered by Rome in the first four centuries of its empire. The first defeat under Varus terminated Roman ambitions in northern Europe and showed first the vulnerability of cavalry in some situations and second its necessity for infantry protection in other circumstances. The second defeat, under the Emperor Valens at Adrianople, put an end to the supremacy of the Roman infantry legion and initiated the era of cavalry domination over infantry. This domination lasted for some 16 centuries, only ending during the First World War.

From the earliest years the Romans had never been entirely happy with cavalry, although they did realize its value. Their most successful general, Julius Caesar, had certainly used Gallic cavalry to very good effect, but it had usually been employed in a supportive role to the legions. Other tribes as well as the Gauls had developed the use of cavalry and, in particular, the tribes living in the wide open spaces of Asia had become highly skilled in cavalry action. At Adrianople the skill was put to very good effect.

The engagement was a consequence of the great migration westward of the Huns (a tribe originating in central Asia), a movement which persisted until the middle of the fifth century. In 378 this migration led in turn to a displacement of the Visigoths, who had settled in the region to the north-west of the Black Sea, across the Danube into the eastern Roman Empire, in the search for a new homeland. Valens, who was not a very effective emperor, decided to drive the Goths back across the Danube. He had been promised help from his co-emperor in the west, his nephew Gratian, but decided to attack the forces of the leader of the Goths, Fritigern, without waiting for additional support. He concentrated his troops in Adrianople, knowing that the enemy was camped just outside the city. The Roman forces, legions and some supporting cavalry, advanced out of the city and encountered Fritigern's wagon camp in a narrow valley. The Gothic cavalry were away from camp on a foraging expedition. Instead of keeping the Roman cavalry close to the legions as flank protection, by some misjudgement they were sent out to meet and attack the returning enemy cavalry. The Roman cavalry were no match for Fritigern's horsemen and were destroyed in the resulting battle. The next day the same cavalry, largely Alans and Sarmatians from Asia, attacked the unprotected legions in confined conditions which prevented proper infantry deployment. The legions were completely destroyed and Valens was killed.

News of the defeat, and of the success of the enemy cavalry, quickly reached Gratian and the rest of the empire, including Britain and Gaul, and here some evidence of the growing appreciation of the importance of cavalry can be seen in the *Notitia Dignitatum*. This document lists the officers of the Roman Empire, both civil and military, and the units they commanded. It is not certain to which year the document refers but the latest estimate puts the probable date around the year 395, some 20 years after Adrianople. In the document three commands are identified in Britain and these reflect the new military organization introduced in the later years of the fourth century. Similar commands are identified across the Channel in Gaul. At this time the Roman armies were reorganized into frontier troops (*limitanei*), which were largely static, and field armies, which were mobile. The frontier troops were planned on an area basis, with each commanded by a *dux* or duke, whereas the field armies were commanded by a *comes* or count. Both were under the command of a *magister militum* or commander-in-chief, although the count took precedence over the duke – the reverse of the modern arrangement.

In Britain, according to the *Notitia*, there was a *dux Britanniarum* based in York, who was in charge of the forces guarding the frontier on Hadrian's Wall, together with their rear support troops. The second command was headed by the *comes litoris Saxonici*, the Count of the Saxon Shore, whose task it was to defend the coast of Britain against the attacks of Saxon raiders. The duties of this count had diminished over the years, for the title in this command was probably originally held by the head of a much wider command, based in an area covering both sides of the Channel in Britain and in Gaul. Such a unit was probably formed in the early years of the fourth century. This early command possibly included *comitatenses* or élite troops, but by the time of the *Notitia* the command was much reduced to a force of *limitanei* smaller than that led by the Duke of the Britains, only the title of count remaining. The Continental responsibilities of the earlier and wider command were taken over by the Dukes of Armorica and Belgica Secunda.

The third command in Britain, and perhaps the most important, included mobile troops able to meet danger coming from any direction. It was headed by the *comes Britanniarum*, the Count of the Britains, and the *Notitia* lists six cavalry and three infantry regiments under his command. Clearly, 20 years after Adrianople, cavalry outnumbered infantry in the field army and the Count of the Britains would not only have been more mobile than Suetonius Paulinus in putting down the insurrection in AD 61 but also no doubt have used very different tactics. It is also interesting to note that one of the cavalry units had the title *equites Honoriani seniores* and was thus in being during the reign of Honorius (395–421). It is therefore likely that forces of the third command, including cavalry, were in Britain up to the time when most of the Roman forces were withdrawn in 407. Their performance and tactics must have been well known to Arthur's grandparents and hence to Arthur some 80 years later.

Although the use of cavalry as the major factor in war originated in the east and spread westwards through the Roman Empire, there was no corresponding appreciation of its value among the northern tribes of Europe. Very few items of horse harness have been found in the burial sites of Angles, Saxons, Jutes or Frisians.

The use of cavalry certainly penetrated throughout the Roman Empire in the later years of the fourth century, but one factor differentiated these cavalry formations from those of the seventh century and later. The stirrup was not introduced to the west until the reign of the Emperor Maurice in the last years of the sixth century. As will be seen later, the absence of this piece of horse harness almost certainly affected the tactics used in British engagements around the year 500.

One other aspect of the cavalry formations mentioned in the *Notitia* is important. There are two possible forms they could take: either heavily armoured units, in which both man and horse are well protected by armour, or light cavalry, relatively unarmoured, in which the emphasis is placed on speed and mobility. The lance, shield and sword would be used by both forms of cavalry but the Roman cavalry sword was not the short sword made famous by the legions, but a longer one, much more effective when used by a man in an elevated position on horseback. Such a sword was probably copied from that used by tribal horsemen enlisted into the Roman armies in the early years of the empire.

Records suggest, however, that heavy cavalry was used only in the eastern empire. In any case, the numbers and skills of armourers declined in the west as the Roman Empire receded after the start of the fifth century and this would militate against the use of heavy cavalry. For these reasons, it is likely that the units mentioned in the *Notitia* were light cavalry formations which would indeed provide the higher degree of mobility needed by the Count of the Britains to move to any part of the coast where danger threatened. This type of cavalry would be remembered in Britain and Gaul throughout the fifth century.

In one other field Roman custom extended to future leaders in later centuries. In several instances in the first four centuries AD, provincial leaders became emperors in their own countries or even in Rome itself. This process became so important in both Britain and Gaul in the fifth century (the century of Arthur's birth) that it is useful to see how the custom started and how it grew in these early centuries.

Members of the ruling élite, from the Julio-Claudian dynasty onwards, whether of Roman or of mixed Roman and provincial descent, quickly realized that it was possible to obtain supreme power through election to Augustus (the senior imperial title) if supported by their own troops. The qualities required for such an individual to succeed were usually wealth, intelligence, charisma and a good measure of political skill. However, one other quality was usually essential: namely, military ability. Any man seeking supreme power in times prior to the development of true democracy would find it valuable to be aware of tried and tested military techniques, as well as the latest developments in tactics and strategy in the field. In the early centuries, the Romans were far in advance of any nation beyond their frontiers in military competence and, in consequence, would-be leaders both inside and outside the empire in those years generally required a sound knowledge of the Roman way in warfare.

Although in the earlier years of the empire the election to emperor often involved the troops in Rome itself – the praetorian guard, for example – in later years provincial troops were involved, sometimes in regions far removed from Rome. When provincial troops elected their own emperor, particularly in the declining years of the empire, such action proved to be one of the causes of imperial disintegration and was an important factor in the formation of the successor states in the west and in the rise of new leaders in those states.

During the first imperial dynasty, the Julio-Claudians, the creation of a new emperor became strongly dependent on military support. The fourth emperor, Claudius, promised the troops 15,000 sesterces per head to support his candidature and set a pattern to be followed by future emperors. After the Julio-Claudian and the Flavian dynasties, two emperors came to power through the process of adoption by their predecessor. These two, Trajan and Hadrian, were both efficient rulers and each had an unusually long reign. In their own persons they set another new precedent for Roman emperors in that their families were provincial, not Roman, both coming from Spain. Neither, however, came to power through military insurrection in the provinces.

The sequence of adoptive emperors continued after Hadrian with Antoninus, who also came from a provincial family, this time in Gaul, and Marcus Aurelius, both excellent rulers who extended the series of good emperors, which started with Trajan in 98, up to the year 180. The series ended with Marcus Aurelius's son Commodus, during whose 12-year reign the authority wielded at the centre of the empire was seriously weakened. At the same time pressure from beyond the frontiers was almost continuous and many legions had to be stationed at considerable distances from Rome. When the central power diminished, there was a temptation for ambitious commanders from these distant parts either to march their troops towards Rome and claim the whole empire or, alternatively, to declare themselves an independent emperor of as many provinces as they could reasonably control.

Such a situation developed shortly after Commodus's death. Three military commanders, Clodius Albinus, governor in Britain, Septimius Severus, commanding in Pannonia, and Pescennius Niger in Syria, all had imperial ambitions and were supported by their respective commands (see Salway 1981: 217). All three started to move towards Rome, but Severus, being the closest, got there first and declared himself emperor. Albinus was then neutralized by the promise of elevation to junior emperor, permitting Severus to defeat Pescennius at Issus in Cilicia. The promise to Albinus did not materialize and consequently he decided to move his troops across the Channel to support his claim by force of arms. He failed, being defeated by Severus near Lyons in 196. This pattern of emperor creation was to be repeated many times in the next 200 years.

The removal of Albinus's troops from the province made Britain more vulnerable to attack and the new governor, Senecio, took the unusual step of asking for the personal help of the emperor in the form of an imperial expedition. Severus welcomed the call and came with his family, including his son Caracalla, who was to become the next emperor. Both Severus and Caracalla campaigned in Britain, following the pattern set by earlier emperors, which would also be continued by some of their successors. Severus died in York in 211.

The Severan dynasty stretched from 193 to the death of Alexander Severus in 235. Thereafter, following a series of short reigns, Gallienus succeeded as sole emperor subsequent to the defeat, capture and imprisonment of his father, Valerian, the co-emperor, at the hands of the Persians. It was under Gallienus that the second major instance of emperor creation in the west occurred. After halting a German invasion of northern Italy at Milan in 258, Gallienus was forced to move eastwards to suppress a rebellion in the Danube provinces. Detecting a weakness at the centre, Postumus, the Roman commander on the Rhine, murdered both the praetorian prefect, Silvanus, and Gallienus's son, Saloninus. Then, in 259, following tradition, he declared himself emperor. On this occasion he did not move on Rome, but decided to form a new empire of the Gallic provinces, having received the support of troops in Germany, Gaul, Spain and Britain. Gallienus also conceded control of the east to Queen Zenobia, the wife of the Roman vice-regent who ruled from Palmyra. It remained to Aurelian, who succeeded in 270, to reunite the empire by force of arms, first reclaiming the west from Tetricus, who had succeeded Postumus and Victorinus as Gallic emperor, at the battle of Châlons in 271, and then defeating Zenobia at Antioch in 272.

These two instances of attempted or actual emperor creation, one in Britain and one in Gaul, set a pattern of power acquisition in these provinces which must have had considerable influence on future potential leaders in this part of the Roman world. The pattern was reinforced by further cases of imperial ambition in both western provinces.

The next case of emperor creation involved both Britain and Gaul and is important for its association with a new system of imperial defence, probably introduced by the Emperor Probus, who succeeded to the imperial title in 276. Throughout the third century the western fringes of the empire were subject to attack by pirates, chiefly Saxons or Franks, on the east and south coasts of Britain and on the north coast of Gaul. The Roman countermeasures had made use of the British fleet, the *classis Britannica,* but the ships available were not capable of continuous patrols of the coastline. An alternative response was called for and provided by the construction of forts along the coasts most at risk. In Britain the two coastal forts at Brancaster and Reculver were augmented by a further seven between Burgh Castle in Norfolk and Portchester in Hampshire. In Gaul forts at Grannona near the mouth of the Seine and at Marcae near Calais were also part of the total defence system. In this way protected havens were created which both facilitated naval patrols and provided military centres capable of repelling invaders, all of which contributed towards solution of the pirate problem. We know from the *Notitia Dignitatum* that these forts in Britain came, at the end of the fourth century, under the control of the Count of the Saxon Shore.

The new system contained the problem but, as usual, the price of safety was continued vigilance. Raids were still attempted after Probus died in 282 and persisted through a succession of ineffective emperors until Diocletian took command in 284. He introduced the concept of the tetrarchy, with two senior emperors given the title of Augustus and the two junior the title of Caesar. This new imperial arrangement started with the appointment of Maximian as Caesar to oversee the west, while Diocletian dealt with eastern affairs. Maximian was immediately successful in suppressing the *Bagaudae*, bands of disaffected peasants and others who were causing widespread trouble in Gaul. This led to his promotion to Augustus and co-ruler with Diocletian in 286, but it was not until 293 that the full complement of four emperors were in post.

There were, however, other immediate western problems that claimed Maximian's attention and, to give him some freedom of action, he appointed an experienced soldier named Carausius to handle the pirate problem, with command of the British fleet and of forces in Britain and northern Gaul. During his anti-piratical campaign, Carausius fell under suspicion of diverting the pirates' ill-gotten gains to himself. Maximian, regarding the case against Carausius as proven, sentenced him to death in his absence. Carausius made the only possible response in order to stay alive: he declared himself emperor of the British provinces in 286 (see Salway 1981: 288). He followed the pattern set by Postumus some 27 years earlier and remained as local emperor, making no move against the centre.

It was not until 296 that Constantius Chlorus, one of the Caesars of the tetrarchy introduced by Diocletian, restored Britain to the empire. In due time Constantius became the Augustus in the west and he, together with his son Constantine, conducted a campaign in Britain to strengthen the northern frontiers. These two repeated the success of Severus and Caracalla some 100 years earlier and, adding to the coincidence, Constantius died in York. Constantine was proclaimed Augustus by the legionary troops in Britain in 306, but it was not until 324 that the tetrarchy ended and Constantine became sole, and the first Christian, emperor, taking the title of Constantine the Great. One of his most important innovations was the creation of a parallel administration centre in the east at his capital city (to be named

Constantinople), which increased the possibility of two entirely separate Roman Empires in the future.

By the start of the fourth century, the pattern of independent imperial control in Britain and Gaul had been well established as a viable and acceptable political system in the west. It was to be further strengthened in both dioceses during the fourth and early fifth centuries.

In the mid-fourth century both Britain and Gaul were subject, as before, to attack from the barbarians of the north-west. The attack in Britain occurred in 367 and great destruction was caused by the invading Picts and Scots. Reacting to this problem, the western emperor, Valentinian, appointed an able general named Theodosius to subdue the Picts and Scots in Britain. This was achieved in a most effective manner, and in the following two years Theodosius carried out a remarkable programme of repairing the damage caused by the invaders. He took his son, also named Theodosius, with him and the younger man gained valuable military experience which stood him in good stead when he later became the Emperor Theodosius the Great. In this way the young Theodosius was following in the footsteps of Caracalla and Constantine, both of whom became emperors after a useful stint as young men with their fathers in Britain. Valentinian was equally successful in re-establishing the frontiers of Gaul on the Rhine. His brother, Valens, emperor in the east, was not so fortunate. He was the emperor mentioned earlier who died at Adrianople, defeated by the eastern barbarian cavalry.

Valentinian died in 375 and was succeeded as western emperor by his son Gratian, whose reign saw the making of an emperor who has been remembered in Welsh literature. Gratian had established his headquarters at Trier and had appointed a soldier, Magnus Maximus by name, to high rank in Britain, possibly as *comes* or *dux*. In 382 he, like Theodosius, gained a victory over the Picts and Scots and, detecting some slackening of authority in Gaul, decided to make a bid for power. In 383 he was elected Augustus by his troops and he then took them across the Channel into Gaul. Gratian, deserted by his forces, fled to Lyons, where he was assassinated. The younger Theodosius, by now emperor in the east, accepted Maximus as Augustus in the west. This did not, however, satisfy Maximus and in 387 he crossed the Alps and captured Milan. Spurred into action, Theodosius moved against him and defeated him twice in Pannonia. The final defeat, at Aquileia in northern Italy in 388, resulted in Maximus's capture and execution.

The memory of Magnus Maximus was retained by the people of

Britain, later to become the Welsh, in *The Mabinogion*, a collection of Celtic stories first written down around 1300. The relevant story is entitled 'The Dream of Macsen Wledig' ('The Dream of Prince Macsen') and is the only one of the *Mabinogion* stories which bears any clear relation to history.

The final cases of emperor creation in Britain and Gaul occurred in the fifth century and are better dealt with in the next chapter, which reviews the history of the period immediately preceding the careers of Arthur and Clovis.

Summarizing, some provincial families supplied Roman emperors, such as Antoninus, whose family came from Gaul. Others were elected by the provincial troops under their command: Albinus, Carausius, Constantine the Great and Magnus Maximus by British forces and Postumus by the forces in Gaul. Finally, three emperors, two of whom became famous, campaigned in Britain with their fathers before their accession as emperor: Caracalla, Constantine the Great and Theodosius the Great. These powerful traditions were passed down through the years by Roman historians or by word of mouth and would probably have inspired fifth-century leaders in both Britain and Gaul to emulate to some degree their illustrious examples.

The last two chapters have outlined the basic traditional, social and military influences which must have been felt in the fifth century by the leaders and peoples of the two western provinces of the Roman Empire, Britain and Gaul. These provinces were originally Celtic tribal kingdoms possessing a Celtic heritage. They were conquered by the Romans and subsequently influenced by their conquerors in all fields of human endeavour, but their Celtic nationhood was by no means submerged.

The life of Magnus Maximus ended in 388, less than 100 years from Arthur's lifetime. From this point, although there was one other British Augustus who almost reached the gates of Rome, imperial influence declined and Celtic influences reappeared and grew. At the same time, the inexorable pressure from the barbarian tribes in northwestern Europe continued and was one of the factors leading ultimately to the collapse of the western Roman Empire.

The effects of these pressures on the development of Britain and Gaul in the late fifth and early sixth centuries will be traced throughout the next three chapters. During this period the sense of parallel development fades and a divergence appears which widens progressively in the later sixth century. The cause of the divergence will be identified with the intervention of two men, Arthur in Britain and Clovis in Gaul.

# Fifth-century History before Arthur and Clovis

AT THE start of the search for the real Arthur, all that could be assumed was that a man of that name existed in Britain at a time falling within the last decades of the fifth century. The evidence for this very limited assumption is clearly set out by Nennius and in the *Annales Cambriae* and is generally accepted as true. The situation is very different in Gaul, where it is universally accepted that Clovis led the Frankish tribes at about the same time and that his conquest of Gaul is historical fact.

Throughout much of what follows, Arthur, lacking at the outset firm historical credentials, will appear as the defender of a fast-disappearing diocese of a decaying Roman Empire. In contrast, Clovis, with an assured place in history, attacks the adjacent diocese, already fragmented, and leads the vigorous growth of the emerging medieval Europe. Despite their positions on opposite sides of the great divide between the old and the new Europe, their achievements, if Arthur's can be proved here, will show similarities.

One other fact is almost certainly true. In addition to the general influences outlined in the two previous chapters, historical events in western Europe during the fifth century must have influenced the lives and behaviour of both men in the last three decades of the fifth century. For this reason the relevant events of the first seven decades of fifth-century history in Britain and Gaul need to be reviewed.

After the defeat of Magnus Maximus in 388, Theodosius the Great faced further rebellion in the west, but by 394 he had reunited the whole empire under his command. His death in 395 marked the start of a century important for the arguments developed here in two respects. In the first place, it initiated the irreversible decline of the western Roman Empire and, secondly, it marked the beginning of the century preceding the lives of both Arthur and Clovis.

In consequence, the history of this century provides the background to the events and situations both men had to face during their lives. This background fell within the experience of their fathers and grandfathers and would be known to each without the need of written records. The family experience would be particularly important to the British leader, since around the year 400 the interest of Continental historians in British affairs faded. The decline in interest was due initially to the difficulties encountered in sending military assistance to Britain in order to counter increased invasion pressures, probably Pictish before 400. When these difficulties became insuperable, the consequence was a major loss of contact between Roman historians and British events. The gap in the historical record was only inadequately replaced by native writers. As a result, the absence of Continental interest in Britain has, to a great extent, restricted our own direct knowledge of the fifth-century history of this island to the limited information available from British sources and from the equally sparse records of the Anglo-Saxon invaders.

As mentioned before, the earliest British source for the fifth century is a text by a monk named Gildas which was written in Wales around the year 540 under the title *On the Ruin of Britain*. Unfortunately, Gildas was more concerned with the religious shortcomings of some of the rulers of Britain than with an unprejudiced history of his times. Nevertheless, although his interests were primarily religious, he does provide a limited historical framework for fifth-century events.

There may also have been other fifth-century writers now unknown. The evidence for this comes from another monk, Nennius, who was probably writing in the first decade of the ninth century. In the preface to his book *History of the British* he writes: 'I have therefore made a heap of all that I have found, both from the annals of the Romans and from the chronicles of the Holy Fathers, and from the writings of the Irish and the English, and out of the traditions of our elders.' Included at the end of the earliest full text of Nennius are the *Annales Cambriae*, yearly summaries of important Welsh events from the year 447 to 953. The importance of the *Annales Cambriae* here lies in the inclusion of two references to Arthur, the first giving support to the Badon references in both Nennius and Gildas and the second making a most useful additional contribution to Arthurian data.

Unlike Gildas, Nennius can be classed as a unique historian of his time. In contrast to most of his contemporaries, he did not attempt to write a narrative history, manipulating his facts to suit his personal concepts. His approach was quite different; he collected and published his sources, or extracts of them, and left an assessment of their value to posterity.

Another source of information on fifth-century affairs is provided by the Venerable Bede. His *Historia Ecclesiastia Gentis Anglorum* (*History of the English Church and People*), completed in the year 731, probably makes him the finest European scholar of his time. In Chapters 9 to 22 of Book 1 he deals with British history from 377 to 447, but then leaves a gap without any records from 447 to the mission of St Augustine to Britain, which he places in 596. In the early British chapters, however, he makes much use of Gildas, even going as far as to use similar phrases (cf. Bede, Chapter 16, Book 1, with Gildas, Chapter 25). In consequence, this duplication limits his value as an independent fifth-century witness. He does at the same time draw on other sources, such as *The Life of St Germanus* by the historian Constantius, and so provides Continental references for some British dates. Correlation between any of these very limited British sources does, of course, lend some confidence to their veracity.

In addition, the British sources are supplemented by the information given in *The Anglo-Saxon Chronicle,* another yearly summary of important events, probably compiled in the Wessex court in the ninth century. Here the entries between the years 449 and 593 are relevant. The *Chronicle* does not make any mention of Arthur, but the omission is not surprising since those who compiled the record in later times knew Arthur, as will be argued, as the most successful defender of Britain against the early ancestors of their own people. Nevertheless, the compilers were not so sophisticated as to distort the timescale deliberately in order to conceal Arthur's influence.

Both Nennius and *The Anglo-Saxon Chronicle* concentrate on events and the actions of individuals, and pay less attention to social and economic factors, but even so they provide useful information and opportunities for correlation between sources. In any case, concentration on events and individuals is more appropriate in this particular century. The economic and social structure of the western Roman Empire was disintegrating and the stabilizing influence of the Roman legions was fading. In consequence, initiative and action on a local or even on a national scale were very dependent on the ability of exceptional men to control events within their own sphere of influence.

These problems of inadequate records do not apply to anything like the same extent in Gaul. During the fifth century there, there was no lack of contact with Rome and, in addition, a competent historian,

Gregory of Tours, in his *History of the Franks*, provides much useful information on Gallic events in the fifth and sixth centuries.

Returning to the events at the start of the fifth century, although Theodosius was, in the end, effectively in control of the whole empire, he ensured final separation by making one son, Honorius, emperor of the west and his other son, Arcadius, emperor of the east. The beginning of the new reigns saw no change in the direction of the barbarian thrust from the north and east towards the west and south. This movement was powered by the eastward expansion of the Huns, who, by 406, had reached the north bank of the Danube as far west as Budapest.

The situation, however, was kept under some control by the efforts of a very able soldier, Stilicho, who was appointed by Theodosius as commander of the field army and as guardian of his two young sons. Stilicho was himself a barbarian, a Vandal by birth, and his command included a substantial number of troops recruited from outside the empire to fight alongside the Roman legions.

In the early years of the fifth century, in 401 and again in 403, Stilicho faced invasions of Italy led by Alaric, a Visigoth and a successor of the Fritigern who defeated Valens at Adrianople. Alaric was, like Stilicho, trained in Roman military techniques and had served under Theodosius as commander of the Gothic cavalry. The invasions were repelled but the action was not pressed to its logical conclusion, which required a total elimination of the Gothic threat. Shortly after this, while Gaul had been denuded of troops to meet Alaric's offensive, the Rhine frontier was breached in 407 by an invasion of Vandals and Suebi, who advanced westwards and, facing little resistance, swept across southern Gaul and crossed the Pyrenees into Spain.

Britain, as well as Gaul and Italy, was under attack. The ability to repel invaders had probably been reduced by the attempts of Magnus Maximus to seize the imperial throne and, taking an obvious advantage, the Picts and Scots had started to harass the land from the north. Gildas records two invasions from this direction after the departure of Magnus Maximus, both of which were repelled but only through the intervention of Roman legions sent from the Continent after appeals from Britain for assistance. The recall of the legions after the second invasion possibly reflects the precautions taken by Stilicho, who was feeling the increasing danger from Alaric nearer home.

In addition to the problems caused by barbarians from beyond the imperial frontiers, instability arose within the empire. There were still military forces left in Britain, confirmed by the recorded fact that mutinies broke out in these forces at about the same time that the Vandals crossed into Gaul in early 407. These mutinies led to the residual British forces elevating to emperor a common soldier named Constantine, who, like Maximus and others before him, decided to move on Rome itself. The time seemed propitious in view of the turmoil caused by the Vandal invasion and the threats from Alaric.

Constantine III, his adopted title, took British troops with him and advanced into Gaul, taking control of that province in 407, the very last imperial expedition to be mounted from Britain and Gaul (see Salway 1981: 428). In the following year Constantine's son, Constans, and a very able British general, Gerontius, consolidated the gains by advancing into Spain and claiming the authority of the new emperor, Constantine III, over all three western dioceses: Britain, Gaul and Spain. Faced with this success, Honorius was forced to recognize Constantine in 409 as joint Augustus in the west. These reverses damaged the relationship between Honorius and Stilicho and led to the latter's execution in the same year.

The situation in the west was becoming chaotic. Honorius, still under Gothic threat, had moved the court from Milan to Ravenna. Constantine had established his administration at Arles and had invaded northern Italy. The German tribes which had crossed Gaul were pressing further into Spain. Due to weakness and muddle in Rome, Alaric sacked the city in 410 and shock waves from this catastrophe spread far and wide.

Under the impact of these events another general, Flavius Constantius, emerged to take the place of Stilicho and to introduce some stability in Ravenna. From this time onwards, the fortunes of Honorius started to improve, whereas those of Constantine started to decline. Constans dismissed Gerontius for failing to control the German invasion of Spain, whereupon the latter declared his independence, detached Spain from Constantine's control and invaded Gaul. Here he defeated and killed Constans. Constantine pulled back from Italy and retreated to Arles, where he was besieged by Flavius.

In the meantime, barbarian pressure was re-emerging in the north, where Britain and Gaul were being attacked. *The Gallic Chronicle* (a record comparable to *The Anglo-Saxon Chronicle*) suggests that, on this occasion, the Saxons were responsible for the invasion of Britain. In Gaul the offensive came from German tribes beyond the Rhine. The chaotic situation nearer home meant that in neither diocese was Honorius able to provide any assistance, although a request for help came from Britain. As a result, local authorities took matters into their own hands.

Action by indigenous forces in Britain and Gaul managed to repel the barbarians, but at the same time the blame for Honorius's failure to help was placed firmly on the shoulders of the local Roman officials, civil and military, and all were expelled from both countries. Britain never came back under Roman control, but in Gaul, due to the final defeat of Constantine by Flavius Constantius and his execution in 411, imperial rule was restored by the year 413.

There can be little doubt that the examples provided by Magnus Maximus and Constantine III reinforced the very powerful concept outlined in Chapter 3: the election of emperors by provincial troops and their subsequent moves against the centre of imperial power in Rome; it also presaged the end of Roman control and influence in the west. This feeling that provincial power could be of sufficient strength at least to take control of the periphery and could also, in favourable circumstances, challenge the imperial power at the centre, almost certainly would have influenced western leaders such as Arthur and Clovis in the later years of the fifth century. The successes of Maximus and Constantine, albeit limited, would be well known to the grandparents of Arthur and Clovis and would be passed on to their grandsons, so reinforcing the precedents set by Albinus, Postumus, Carausius and Constantine the Great.

The suffering experienced by Britain and Gaul in the first decade of the fifth century continued intermittently in the years that followed, for there was no end to the barbarian expansion westwards. Indeed, during most of the century both countries were continually harassed by enemies driven westwards by pressures from Hun expansion from the east, which was taking advantage of the power vacuum being created by the decaying Roman Empire in the west.

Alaric died shortly after the sack of Rome and was succeeded by his brother Athaulf, who took his troops out of Italy into Gaul and finally southwards into Spain, where he also died. After his death, Flavius Constantius persuaded the Visigoths to leave Spain and settle in Aquitaine in southern Gaul. Once again, Gaul had been invaded and this time alien tribes had been allowed by Rome to settle in the south-west of the country.

The situation in Britain was somewhat different in that little major barbarian settlement occurred in the first decade of the century. According to Professor Sheppard Frere the sequence of Saxon attack in 408; failure to respond by the officers left behind by Constantine III and their consequent expulsion; British retaliation and success in repelling the invaders; British report to Honorius in Rome in 410, coupled with an appeal for support; rejection of appeal by Honorius – fits the known facts very reasonably (see Frere 1987: 359). However, after 410 little is known of British history until the third decade of the fifth century, and even then detailed information is scarce and there is an increasing dependence on Gildas and Nennius, supported by limited Continental references.

When Honorius remitted the responsibility for British defence to the British in 410, he wrote to the local councils (*civitates*) and not to either the Roman administrators or the military leaders, confirming that Roman control had been lost by that date. Probably the first mention of an emergent British leader is made by Gildas when he refers to 'the members of the [British] council together with the proud tyrant' inviting the Saxons to Britain.

As is very usual with Gildas, he does not give the leader a name but follows the historian Procopius, who uses the word 'tyrant' to describe all the rulers of Britain after the Roman expulsion. A name is, however, provided in two other sources. Nennius calls the ruler in Britain Vortigern and dates the start of his reign as 425 (in the consulship of Theodosius and Valentinian). The ruler's name also appears in *The Anglo-Saxon Chronicle*, which reports that in 455 (the date can be only approximate) the British king, Wurtgern (Vortigern), fought against Hengist and Horsa at Aylesford. There is still a query as to the ruler's actual name, for in the British tongue the word 'Vortigern' means 'high king' and consequently both Nennius and the *Chronicle* may just be giving Gildas's tyrant another title.

In the sentence in Chapter 31 of 'The Kentish Chronicle' in Nennius which first gives Vortigern's name, Nennius also provides valuable information on his reign. He states that the high king 'was under pressure from fear of the Picts and the Scots, and of a Roman invasion, and, not least, from dread of Ambrosius'. This statement is most useful, linking, as it does, British history with three important factors which Vortigern had to consider: first, barbarian invasion: second, Roman affairs; and, third, internal politics. These three factors can be correlated with reliable historical records to substantiate Nennius's account. The correlation also provides a framework for events in the early years of the century preceding the Arthurian period and is therefore of great interest.

The fear of a Roman invasion was perhaps the most serious of the pressures facing Vortigern. The nature of the threat can be associated with events taking place on the Continent. In 421 Honorius had elevated his successful general, Flavius Constantius, to the rank of

Augustus with the name Constantius III. Honorius had also agreed to the marriage of his half-sister, Galla Placidia, to the new Augustus. Constantius III reigned for only a very short time, but the couple had a son, Valentinian, born in 419. Honorius himself died in 423 and was succeeded first by the usurper John, who retained power for only two years, and finally, in 425, by Valentinian III, who was then only a boy of six but still the legitimate heir. His mother, Galla Placidia, acted as regent for him for 25 years.

Placidia found herself in the same position as did Honorius at the start of his reign: she needed a strong and capable soldier for both advice and action if required. She found such a man in Aetius, the *magister militum* or commander-in-chief in Gaul. He had a strong force of barbarians, including Huns, under his command and had forged a considerable reputation. So impregnable had his position become that he was promoted to the rank of 'patrician' in 429, just four years after Vortigern took command in Britain. The rank was a new one; the first to hold the title had been Placidia's husband, Flavius Constantius, but the name itself was derived from that of the ruling class in the earliest days of the Roman republic.

Aetius was an ambitious man and Vortigern might well have feared that the rising soldier would welcome the chance of a Roman triumph which would certainly follow the reconquest of Britain. The writer of 'The Kentish Chronicle' in the collection of historical data which Nennius made clearly knew how events in Rome and Gaul could affect the British situation.

From his comment on the pressures facing Vortigern, the writer probably knew of the Saxon threat in 408, which the British had countered without Roman assistance. He also knew that the Picts and Scots were still causing trouble. In this connection, he was at one with Gildas, for, as mentioned earlier, Gildas reported two invasions of these tribes after the imperial adventure of Magnus Maximus, both repelled with the assistance of Rome. Gildas also reports a third invasion (Chapter 20), but dates it wrongly. He associates the third Pictish invasion with an appeal for help to Aetius (Agitius) in his third consulship – that is, in 446. This date is far too late for major trouble from the Picts; by 446 the Saxons were the main aggressors. It is quite possible that the third Pictish war occurred much earlier, in the gap between 410 and Vortigern's accession. Even so, the northern danger was still felt in the early years of Vortigern's reign, and this also supports the value of Nennius's record.

Some additional evidence to confirm the threat from the north may be deduced from the visit of Germanus, Bishop of Auxerre and former soldier, who had been sent to Britain to root out a Christian heresy initiated by Pelagius, a British theologian who had died in the early years of the fifth century. While he was in Britain, Germanus volunteered to lead a military expedition against invaders in the north or north-west, possibly Picts, and he defeated them. His biographer, a Continental historian named Constantius, dates this engagement precisely to the year 429.

These two factors – the threat from the north, compounded by the fear of Roman reconquest – could well be the cause of Vortigern's welcome, reported in 'The Kentish Chronicle' in Nennius, to the three ships from Germany bringing Hengist and Horsa to Thanet in Kent, Vortigern could be attempting to collect allies who would support Britain against either the Picts or the Romans. Gildas also reports the advent of the three ships, but once again does not provide any names.

The Chronographer in Nennius places the arrival of the Saxons in 428 (both Nennius and Gildas use the name Saxon as a collective noun to include all the tribes invading from the Continent: Saxons, Angles, Jutes and others). 'The Kentish Chronicle' notes that Vortigern allowed the invaders to settle in the island of Thanet. Gildas gives no date for the invasion and records only that the Saxons 'on the orders of the ill-fated tyrant . . . fixed their dreadful claws on the east side of the island'. Both historians agree that some sort of bargain was struck between Vortigern and the Saxons to exchange support in return for supplies. In Nennius the support is said to be against Vortigern's (unspecified) enemies, in Gildas it is 'to beat back the peoples of the north'. These two pressures on Vortigern, from the Romans and the Picts, coupled with his responses to them, set the pattern of political realities in the first years of his reign.

The third pressure on Vortigern was of a more personal nature. The prominence given by Nennius to Vortigern's dread of Ambrosius is not specifically mentioned by Gildas. There is, however, a link in Gildas which not only fits in with the Nennius reference to Ambrosius but is also crucial to understanding the sequence of events in Britain in the fifth century. Fortunately, the relevant part of Gildas's work is, this time, not obscured by his strong religious sentiments. It is a straightforward, matter-of-fact statement which helps to place the Ambrosius family in chronological order.

It is generally agreed that Gildas wrote his book in about 540, and in it he states his own age to be 43. In a vitally important paragraph he names one very successful British leader as Ambrosius Aurelianus and tells us that 'his descendants in our day [540] have become greatly inferior to their grandfather's excellence'. Since Gildas, like most authors, imagines his readers to be about the same age as himself, he is claiming that his own grandfather was a contemporary of Ambrosius Aurelianus. Gildas's father was certainly active in the last decade of the fifth century, when Gildas was born, and his grandfather, a generation earlier, would have been active around 470. Consequently, it is possible to place the success of Ambrosius Aurelianus around 470. It is then possible to place Ambrosius Aurelianus's birth probably some 30 or 40 years earlier, between 430 and 440. So, the parents of Ambrosius Aurelianus would be contemporaries of Vortigern, who had become High King in 425. Gildas notes that these parents 'who had worn the purple, were slain in it'.

It is thus almost certain that the Ambrosius whom Vortigern dreaded was an influential British leader, clearly an opponent of his, and the father of the Ambrosius Aurelianus so admired by Gildas. It is very possible that the Elder Ambrosius had been elected by the British army 'to wear the purple', as many generals before had been. The Elder Ambrosius could then have been the leader of a faction which hoped to restore Roman prestige and power to Britain. He was no doubt inspired by the examples of Magnus Maximus and Constantine III, who both, within the memory of older people, had also been elected by the British army to 'wear the purple'. The Elder Ambrosius would almost certainly have known of Carausius, who became the provincial emperor of Britain in 286.

Vortigern, on the other hand, represented a tendency to support a more Celtic type of society. His position as High King, as his name implies, indicated a reversion to a pre-Roman social structure and his authority over a number of petty kings conforms with the purely Celtic development of society in Ireland, which had totally escaped Roman aggression.

The 'pressure' sentence in Nennius does therefore correlate well with reliable historical facts in both Continental references and Gildas. This consequently supports the accuracy and value of the collection – at least in those parts which are clearly not derived from folklore or myth.

As a result of these references to British leaders, Gildas and Nennius have between them provided a reasonable dated framework for some British events in the first half of the fifth century. There is also a degree of agreement between them, and this gives mutual support to the status of both as being reliable in at least parts of their texts.

A further confirmation of the sequence of events is provided by the Nennius Chronographer when he records that 'from the [beginning of the] reign of Vortigern to the quarrel between Vitalinus and Ambrosius are twelve years that is Wallop, the battle of Wallop'. Vitalinus could be either an ally of Vortigern or the actual name of Vortigern, the High King. In consequence of this statement, it is clear that 'dread of Ambrosius' was still being felt by Vortigern in 437, 12 years after his accession in 425, and the Elder Ambrosius was alive in that year. He could, therefore, have fathered Ambrosius Aurelianus in the 430s. The battle of Wallop also indicates that conditions in Britain between 410 and 440 were still very unsettled; the country was suffering from the effects of both civil war and barbarian invasion.

It is probable that Gildas's view of Vortigern's character, using such words as 'proud' or 'ill-fated', is biased by the author's tendency, as already mentioned, to judge leaders on their moral and religious shortcomings rather than on political or military success. Nennius, on the other hand, takes a more dispassionate approach and shows Vortigern to be a man with many problems as the leader of the successor state which followed the collapse of Roman authority. Vortigern, in the Nennius record, reacts as a politician to the pressures he faced. His initial welcome to the Saxons gained him an ally against the northern invaders, leaving him free to face any attempt by an all-conquering Aetius to cross the Channel and reconquer Britain. The invitation to the Saxons would also enable Vortigern to devote more time and energy to pursue his action against the Elder Ambrosius if the Roman threat did not materialize.

From the start of the fifth century up to the time Vortigern was making his pact with the Saxons and fighting his civil war with Ambrosius, the situation in Gaul was equally unstable. The chief factors affecting the stability were the movements of the British army under Constantine III from north to south in the first decade of the century and of the Visigoth army southward into Spain in the second decade, followed by the latter's settlement in Aquitaine. The invasions continued: the Franks under Clodian moved from their homelands round the mouth of the Rhine towards the mouth of the Somme, the Alemanni crossed into Alsace and the Burgundians, who had founded their kingdom round Worms, were also moving south to the upper Loire and the valley of the Rhône. The movements of all these peoples were probably influenced by the growing threat from the invasion of eastern Europe by the Huns. They did not, however, go unopposed.

During this resurgence of barbarian activity the increasing power and military expertise of Aetius became apparent. In battles in 435 and 436 he imposed crushing defeats on the two most serious invaders, the Burgundians and the Franks, but he did not expel them. He took an alternative course, which was willingly accepted by the tribes he conquered, of attempting to absorb these peoples into the western Roman Empire and recruiting their menfolk into the Roman army. Following these successes, Aetius continued his policy of attempting to stabilize the Gallic diocese, both to augment his own personal power and to increase his influence with the regent, Galla Placidia. In 442 he settled the Alans in the Loire region, with some opposition from the local inhabitants, and in the following year he created a new kingdom for the Burgundians in the Savoy – in both cases a more satisfactory arrangement than Vortigern managed to make with the Saxons in Britain.

Reverting to British affairs, the Chronographer in Nennius records the arrival of the Saxons in 428, which marked the prelude to the invasion of Britain. At first they were welcomed as possible allies against either Picts or Romans, but they were never needed against the latter.

As mentioned earlier, both Nennius and Gildas agree that Vortigern made a bargain with the Saxons. He promised to grant supplies and in return he required the Saxons 'to fight bravely against his enemies' (Nennius) or 'to fight for our country' (Gildas). It seems that the Saxons kept their part of the bargain – there were no further successful Pictish raids. Again, both Nennius and Gildas agree that the British broke the agreement by withholding the supplies. This action was a major error of judgement on Vortigern's part, for the consequences were disastrous.

At this point Nennius drifts off into a series of apocryphal stories, but Gildas describes the events after the treaty break quite explicitly. He reports that the Saxon response was to threaten to 'plunder the whole island unless more lavish payments' were made. No supplies were received and the threat was put into immediate practice. There follows a graphic account by Gildas of the terror and devastation which resulted from the great raid of the Saxons, which penetrated almost to the west coast of the island (see Map 1 on page 64). He records: 'All the major towns were laid low . . . the foundation stones of high walls and towers had been torn down . . . there was rarely to be seen grape-cluster or corn-ear.'

It is important to date this first major aggression by the invaders from the Continent. According to *The Gallic Chronicle*, it was in 440 that 'Britain, abandoned by the Romans, passed into the power of the Saxons'. This coincided with the defeats Aetius was imposing on the barbarian invaders of Gaul. *The Gallic Chronicle* was, however, a little

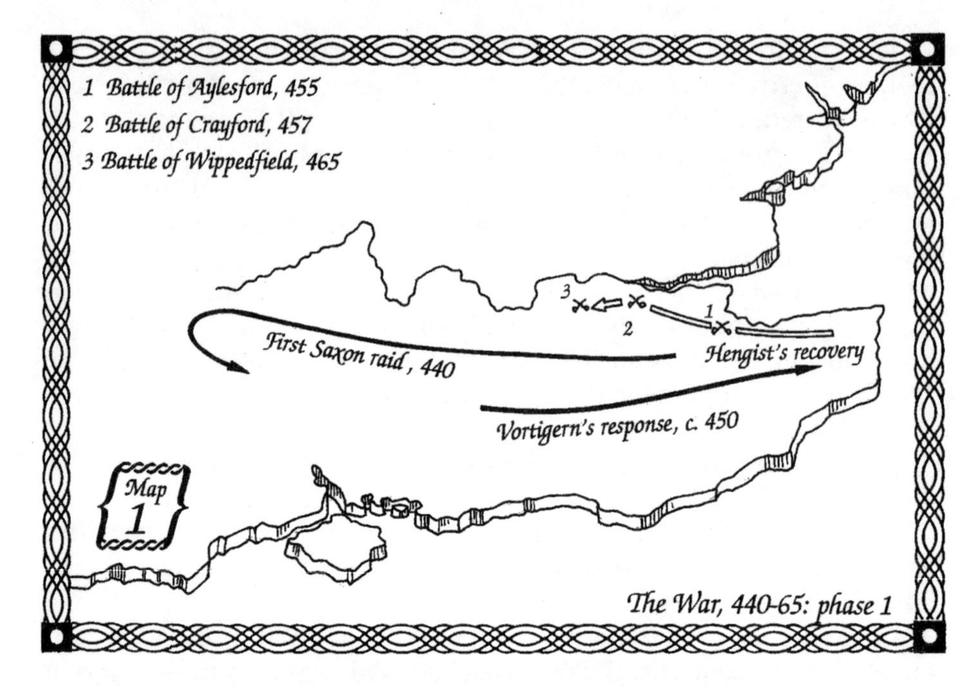


premature for Gildas goes on to say that 'after a time, when the cruel plunderers had gone home', there was a British revival.

Gildas also records that, before the revival, another result of the raid was a British emigration 'beyond the sea'. This refers to the British settlements in Armorica (Brittany) and further eastwards along the north coast of Gaul. The emigrants after the Saxon raid joined the British remnants of the army of Magnus Maximus or Constantine III who had never returned to the land of their birth. Some evidence for this migration can be found in British place-names in Brittany and Normandy.

It is possible that the account by Gildas of the raid and the recovery sequel covers quite a number of years, longer than the text perhaps suggests. Confirmation of the date in *The Gallic Chronicle* for the start of the raid in 440 is provided by Gildas when he records the appeal for help to Aetius in 446 (he mistakenly attributed the reason for the appeal to Pictish danger). This appeal failed in that no military assistance was provided, for, as indicated earlier, Aetius was otherwise engaged. He may, however, have authorized a second visit of St Germanus in 446/7 as some sort of response. Taken together, the appeal and the note in *The Gallic Chronicle* make it fairly certain that the raid can be dated to the years between 440 and 446.

This raid marks the start of the Anglo-Saxon conquest of Britain. The whole conquest can conveniently and naturally be divided into some six phases (see Appendix 3) and the raid itself, together with the period of British recovery after the raid, constitutes the first phase or component of the conquest sequence. The later phases will be discussed in Chapter 6, but the first is better considered here, for it occurred well before the start of the careers of both Arthur and Clovis.

At the outset it is essential to consider a discrepancy between corresponding dates in Nennius and *The Anglo-Saxon Chronicle* for the first arrival of the invaders. In the former, Hengist's arrival is placed in 428, three years after Vortigern's accession in 425; in the latter the arrival occurs 21 years later, in 449. This is the first of only two instances where a major discrepancy has to be addressed in *The Anglo-Saxon Chronicle* within the period of the conquest sequence. In this case, the *Chronicle* date cannot be fitted satisfactorily into a logical and smooth sequence.

It is important to settle the matter since the *Chronicle* date of 449 for the arrival of Hengist is later than both the Gallic date for his victory in 440 and the British appeal to Aetius for help in 446. A resolution of this problem can be found by looking at the time interval between Vortigern's invitation to the 'Saxons' and the end of the first stage of British recovery, which is conveniently placed by the *Chronicle* in 455, at the battle of Aylesford between Vortigern and Hengist. The time intervals are therefore 27 years in Nennius but only six years in the *Chronicle.*

When these intervals are examined, it will be seen that they start, in both records, with Vortigern's invitation to the invaders to help the British. Both records also agree that the help degenerated into conflict after the invaders were reinforced from the Continent. No other information is given by the *Chronicle* to fill the six-year interval apart from a specific claim of more than one Saxon victory over the Picts. However, in Nennius, Gildas and Continental references, many more events are recorded to fill the 27-year interval. There are first the two visits of St Germanus in 429 and 446/7. Second, as a result of the invitation to the Saxons, there is evidence that the threat from the Picts was removed. Third, it is also during this interval that the civil war developed between Vortigern and Ambrosius the Elder. The start was possibly indicated by the battle of Wallop in 437, but there is no indication that the Elder Ambrosius died in the battle. He was, however, 'slain in the purple' at a later date and consequently the civil war was probably still in progress after the Saxon great raid to the west. Fourth, the interval includes this raid westwards, the resulting destruction and the consequent emigration of many British to northern Gaul. Finally, after this, a British campaign must have been planned and executed to result in an advance of British forces eastwards, for both the *Chronicle* and Nennius next report battles in Kent (starting in 455, according to the *Chronicle*) and led by Vortigern and his son Vortimer.

The few events recorded in the *Chronicle*, on the one hand, and the amount of real information included in Nennius's and Gildas's accounts, on the other, all suggest that the latter are more reliable in this instance and that a 27-year interval is needed to accommodate all the events. Consequently, a Saxon arrival date of 428 is to be preferred. However, as will be argued consistently later, this date for the first advent of the invaders is possibly the only instance of a major event error in *Chronicle* dating during the fifth and sixth centuries.

Within this first phase of the conquest of Britain, the first stage of British recovery is marked by the Kentish battles, which showed almost complete recovery following the great Saxon raid to the west. The *Chronicle* lists three victories in battle against the British in the Kent area between 455 and 465. The first was in 455 at Aylesford, where Horsa, the brother of Hengist, was killed; the second was in 457 at Crayford; and the third was in 465 near 'Wippedfleet' (possibly just south of London). This account coincides with an undated record in Nennius (Chapter 44), which also describes three battles where the British leader was Vortimer, the son of Vortigern, and the enemy was 'Hengist and Horsa and their people'. In his account, Nennius reports that the British were the victors throughout and that in one battle, at Episford (Aylesford), Horsa was killed.

It is probable that the battles described in Nennius are the same as those recorded in the *Chronicle* since the death of Horsa is mentioned in both accounts. Consequently, although there is disagreement on the victors, there is confirmation from two sources that, after the first major thrust west, the progress of recovery had pushed the frontier between British and Saxon back towards the east of the island.

The problem of the victorious side in Kent will be further examined in Chapter 6, but here, on the basis of the battle list sequence in the *Chronicle*, it is suggested that the British revival had overreached itself. Hengist was again moving westwards towards London. The British had probably penetrated too far into the invaders' bridgehead in Kent, for Nennius tells us that Vortimer had besieged the invaders three times in the island of Thanet. Thereafter, Hengist again had taken the initiative and was advancing westward from Aylesford through Crayford to south London to regain control of the south bank of the Thames (see Map 1 on page 64).

The concept of a British advance eastwards far into Kent is also supported by implication in *The Anglo-Saxon Chronicle*. There it is claimed that the Saxons were invited 'to support the Britons' and that Vortigern 'directed them to fight against the Picts' and 'they did so; and obtained the victory'. This claim implies that the Saxons were fighting to the north or north-west of London. However, the next record in the *Chronicle* shows a Saxon advance westwards from Aylesford to Crayford in 455–7 and this requires first a retreat or withdrawal of the Saxons into the east of Kent after the Pictish victories they claimed. As a result, the *Chronicle* supports both Nennius and Gildas in their descriptions of a British revival, particularly since the first two specifically indicate a retreat by the invaders into Kent.

According to Nennius, Vortimer died soon after the Kentish battles and, after treachery at a peace conference called by Hengist, further territorial concessions in Essex, Middlesex and Sussex were forced on Vortigern. There is no other confirmation for this conference, which may be legendary.

The death of Vortigern probably occurred at some time between 465 and 470 and his reign must be regarded as only partially successful. His political initiatives had certainly eliminated danger from the northern invaders but had resulted in the intervention of an even more dangerous invader in the east. There was an explosion of conflict between Hengist and Vortigern which resulted in great damage to Britain and much loss of territory. However, Vortigern and his son Vortimer managed to effect a noteworthy revival, recovering much of the ground lost in the great raid, although it left the invaders in complete control of Kent. After Vortigern's death there is no evidence that the British ever regained control in the south-east. One consequence of Vortigern's failure to anticipate Hengist's aggressive intentions, and perhaps of Vortimer's early death, was the fact that none of Vortigern's sons succeeded him as High King. Nennius names Ambrosius as the next High King (Chapter 48), and this conclusion to the first major aggression of the Anglo-Saxons suggests a deceleration of the return to Celtic values in Britain and a partial restoration of Roman influence.

The Ambrosius named by Nennius as High King was almost certainly the man referred to by Gildas as Ambrosius Aurelianus, the son of the Elder Ambrosius, Vortigern's old enemy. Gildas reports that this Elder Ambrosius and his wife lost their lives in the civil war between the two British factions at some time after the battle of Wallop and before the death of Vortigern. Consequently, the accounts of both Gildas and Nennius coincide in suggesting that the second stage of British recovery, which ended the first phase of the conquest, was in the hands of the Younger Ambrosius, probably from the late 460s onwards. If he remained in charge until the mid 480s, he would then, on the argument presented here, be between 50 and 60, and probably nearing the end of his active life.

While Britain was suffering the first serious invasion of the island since the Roman conquest some 400 years earlier, the situation in Gaul was relatively stable, due to the abilities of Aetius as a military leader. In the early stages of the British struggle with the Saxons, there had been an appeal from Britain to Aetius for help (the one reported by Gildas and, by his error, placed in the context of the third Pictish war). This appeal in, or shortly after, 446 was rejected. In all probability it did not come from Vortigern, in view of his fear of a Roman reconquest, his Celtic leanings and his political inclination to re-establish an understanding with the Saxons. It may well have come from the leader of the Roman faction, the Elder Ambrosius. In any case the appeal did not result in any military assistance.

Aetius's reluctance to help the British, possibly caused by his involvements with the Franks, Burgundians and Alans, may also have been compounded by a danger developing in the east. Attila the Hun, after defeats inflicted on the eastern Roman armies, had decided to move westwards. In 451, with considerable forces at his command, he entered Gaul. He was opposed by Aetius, with a composite army including Franks and Visigoths as well as regular Roman legions. The two armies met on the Catalaunian Plains near Châlons-sur-Marne and, although the result was not entirely conclusive, Attila retreated into Italy, dying there two years later. In 454, mirroring the end of the Stilicho–Honorius partnership, Aetius was murdered by Valentinian III, who had ended the regentship of his mother, Galla Placidia, but was himself assassinated shortly afterwards.

From the mid-century onwards, information relating to the events in Gaul is reasonably well known. A series of western emperors followed Valentinian III, none ruling for more than a few years at most and nearly all ineffectual. However, one of these, Avitus, made a very important appointment: a soldier named Aegidius was made *magister militum* in northern Gaul.

Avitus's hold on imperial power was soon terminated. In 457 he was dismissed from office by Ricimer, a Suebian German who had become a patrician and commander-in-chief. The new military leader was a third in the mould of Stilicho and Aetius, and he dominated the western scene for some 16 years. Both Ricimer and Aegidius were strong characters and in the end they clashed. Although Aegidius was dismissed from office, it proved impossible to make the dismissal effective. Northern Gaul moved out of imperial Roman control and Aegidius founded a separate semi-Roman state in that part of Gaul facing Britain across the Channel. He established his capital at Soissons. In consequence, although northern Gaul had moved outside direct imperial control, most of the country still remained under Roman influence.

Thus, in the third quarter of the fifth century, two similar situations had developed in the two former western Roman dioceses. In Gaul Aegidius had created, in classic fashion, a separate quasi-Roman state following the example of Postumus and Carausius some two centuries earlier. There is little doubt that, as a *magister militum,* he made full use of all the accumulated military knowledge summarized in Chapter 3 and, in his dealings with Ricimer and his neighbours in northern Gaul, use of all the Roman political expertise as well. Central and southern Gaul, apart from the Visigoth south-west, remained under diminishing Roman influence.

In Britain, to parallel Aegidius's achievement, Ambrosius Aurelianus had emerged as High King out of the chaos of invasion and civil war between Celtic and Roman factions. His accession probably happened a few years after Aegidius had been succeeded by his son Syagrius. Judged by his success, Ambrosius had to some extent reconciled the two societies in Britain, the pro-Celtic and the pro-Roman. He, like Aegidius, was probably more committed to Roman influences, but both were quite independent of any imperial control from the western Roman state. Unlike Aegidius, however, Ambrosius was the High King and not a *magister militum* and had still to take account of the growing reversion to a Celtic form of society which was gradually supplanting the Roman.

There were other, more important differences between the positions of Ambrosius and Aegidius, for the former was facing a barbarian threat which had not been eliminated. The Saxons (or perhaps, more accurately, Jutes) were still in secure bridgeheads in Kent and had possibly expanded into the surrounding areas. Although there is no documentary evidence of the invasion of Norfolk and Lincolnshire, there is archaeological evidence from cemeteries that Anglian occupation took place in the early fifth century. There is no evidence of these invaders ever being dislodged, at least from Norfolk. There is also no evidence of friendship between Ambrosius and any of the invaders; indeed, Gildas implies a continuous struggle as 'victory went now to our countrymen, now to their enemies'.

Aegidius, on the other hand, had reasonably amicable relations with his neighbours to the east and to the west. Childeric, King of the Franks, who was on his eastern boundary, had no quarrel with Aegidius, nor had Riothamus, King of Armorica and of the Britons, who had emigrated to north-western Gaul after the first major Saxon advance in the mid-440s. However, around 464 Aegidius died and his son Syagrius inherited what had become known as the Kingdom of Soissons. This change in leadership was to have momentous consequences later in the century.

It is also probable that the campaigns of Hengist against Vortigern and his sons caused great disruption of civilian life in the south of Britain. Such disruption did not occur to the same extent in northern Gaul. Although the Visigoths had settled in the south-west and the Burgundians in the upper Rhône valley, Aegidius had developed a Roman type of authority in north-central Gaul which had ensured some degree of stability there.

The residual western Roman Empire still controlled Provence, and there was some reconciliation between Rome and northern Gaul after Syagrius inherited the Kingdom of Soissons. When the Visigoths in south-western Gaul turned against Roman control, Ricimer and the current emperor, Anthemius, organized a force to restore Roman authority. This included some of the troops formerly under the command of Aegidius and now led by a *comes*, Paulus, together with a contingent of Armoricans and Britons led by Riothamus, the King of Armorica. The effort was unsuccessful but it did demonstrate at least a partial restoration of Roman solidarity and it also indicated relative stability in the northern kingdom, which could clearly afford to send troops over the frontier to assist a distant ally against an aggressive neighbour to the south-west. In these early years of Syagrius's reign, it is interesting to note that he had not taken full command of his troops and, even in later years, he never achieved the military authority held by his father.

Little is known, beyond the sparse detail provided by Gildas, of the activities of Ambrosius Aurelianus during his years as High King, years corresponding very closely with the years in which Syagrius ruled from Soissons. There is, however, one notable piece of research which throws some light on a possible course of action which Ambrosius may have followed in southern Britain after Vortigern's death.

The work was undertaken by Dr John Morris. He notes that army units often bore the name of the emperor who raised them and that such units also named the places where they were garrisoned (see Morris 1973:100). Consequently, military units raised by Ambrosius to prevent further encroachment of the invaders would be named Ambrosiaci and their garrison sites might well bear the prefix Amb–. In addition to five West Country recruiting sites, Morris identified 12 others in more strategic positions. More than half of these were in places important for the protection they could afford to Colchester and London and the rest were in positions to protect the south coast. These latter stretched in an arc from Amesbury in the west to the Medway in the east (See Map 2 below). Amesbury and other similar names such as Ambrosden and Amberley have no English origin and are found only in the south of the island.

Some corroboration of this hypothesis is provided by *The Anglo-Saxon Chronicle,* which, as will be described later in the second and fourth phases of the conquest, reports little penetration inland for many years. Clearly, Ambrosius's protective arc was effective in containing the Saxons along the coast of Sussex and Hampshire. In addition, as will also be shown later, his recruitment sites were effective in containing the Angles north of Colchester. This establishment of recruiting centres by Ambrosius completed the second stage of British recovery after the westward raid in the 440s. It also marked the end of the first phase in the conquest of Britain.

The events in this chapter have taken the history of Britain and northern Gaul as far as the 480s. The leaders of the two countries at

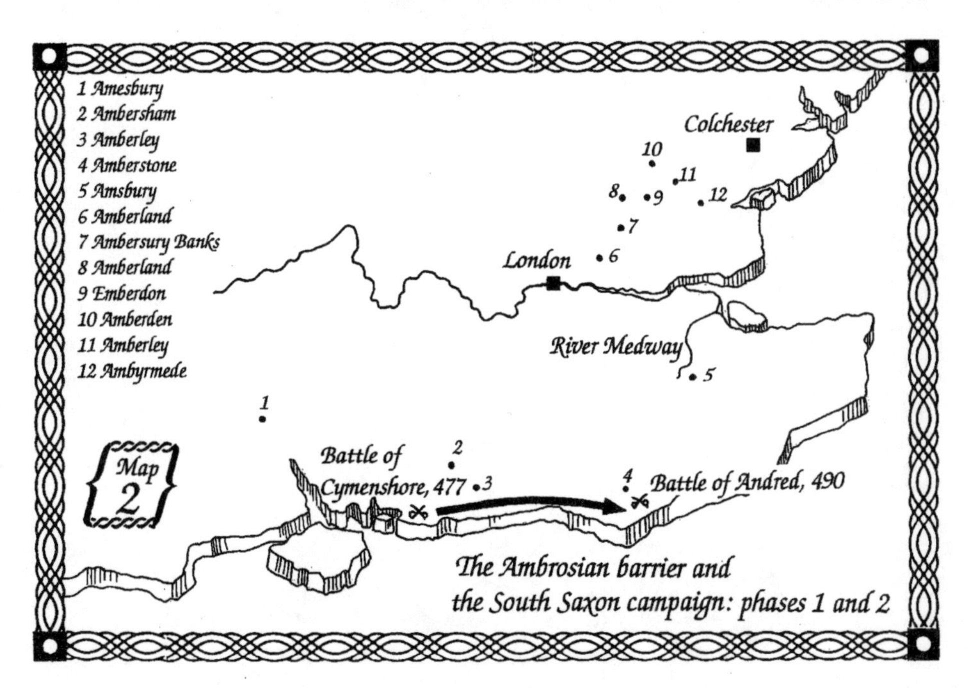


The Ambrosian barrier and the South Saxon campaign: phases 1 and 2

that time were, respectively, Ambrosius and Syagrius, both of whom were to end their careers in the last two decades of the century, the former probably, the latter certainly. Both men had backgrounds which were more Roman than Celtic. Their fathers had been Roman commanders: the Elder Ambrosius had 'worn the purple' and Aegidius was a *magister militum*. Both faced potential enemies from the east. Most of Britain and Gaul still remained under some Roman influence and both countries remained on parallel lines of development. This was not, however, to continue for very much longer.

It is not possible to give any precise date for the end of Ambrosius's reign as High King, but earlier arguments suggest he must have been at least between 50 and 60 in the 480s – a very good age in those early centuries. In northern Gaul the death of Childeric, King of the Franks, in 481 and the accession of his son Clovis swept Syagrius from the scene and led to a parting of the ways between Gaul and Britain. The trend of history in both Gaul and Britain in the latter years of the fifth century and in the sixth century will be considered in the next two chapters.

It is at the start of this period that the influence of Clovis proved vital in determining the future of France. It is here also that arguments will be advanced to show that Arthur played an equally important role in the transformation of Britain into England.

# Conquest and Post-conquest in Gaul

OWING TO the geographical proximity of Gaul and Italy and to the historian Gregory of Tours, the direction taken by Gaul in the last three decades of the fifth century is relatively well documented. Under Aegidius northern Gaul had moved outside the control of the western Roman Empire and stayed outside when Syagrius succeeded his father in 464. Between 464 and the end of the century, the history of Gaul underwent a decisive change and, at the same time, the western Roman Empire collapsed and the Kingdom of Italy came into existence. Both these changes profoundly affected the development of Gaul in the sixth century.

The founding of the new Italy will be considered first. The end of the empire was heralded by the death of Ricimer in 472. He was succeeded as commander-in-chief of the forces of the western Roman Empire first by Orestes and finally by Odoacer in 476. These three military leaders demonstrated the ever-increasing power of the commanders-in-chief, in the pattern of Stilicho and Aetius, and the ever-decreasing power of the emperors. All three had, as commanding generals, supported a series of largely ineffectual western emperors while retaining real authority for themselves. In 476 Odoacer ended this practice and forthwith deposed the last western emperor, Romulus Augustulus, and appointed himself King of Italy. At the same time, he acknowledged a somewhat vague supra-national control exercised by Zeno, the eastern emperor ruling from Constantinople.

One of the reasons for Zeno's acceptance of Odoacer in place of his co-emperor Romulus lay in the fact that the Ostrogoths, under several vigorous leaders, dominated the north-western route from Constantinople to Italy and harried the eastern empire across its northern frontier. Zeno's preoccupation with the Ostrogoths helped to keep

Odoacer secure on the throne of Italy for 13 years. When, however, the Ostrogoths coalesced under a single leader, an intelligent soldier named Theodoric, their pressure on Zeno became intolerable. With a diplomatic stroke which anticipated Machiavelli by many centuries, Zeno commissioned Theodoric to attack and eliminate Odoacer. The commission was accepted, the Ostrogoths turned westwards and the threat to the eastern empire was removed.

Zeno no doubt hoped that the clash between Theodoric and Odoacer would last for many years and that both would be weakened by the trial of strength. The most satisfactory result for Zeno would have been that, at the end of their struggle, neither could pose any threat to the east. He did not, however, take account of the exceptional abilities of Theodoric, who in 489 marched westwards and met Odoacer on the River Isonzo at the head of the Venetian Gulf. The result was a complete victory for Theodoric. This was followed up by an even more decisive victory at Verona, after which Odoacer fled to Ravenna, there to be blockaded until he surrendered in 493 and was killed by Theodoric's own hand. Theodoric took Odoacer's title of King of Italy and his reign lasted for 33 years, providing a relatively stable regime there, in contrast with the violent changes in Britain and Gaul in the latter years of the fifth century. At the turn of the century the influence of Italy on Gallic affairs was due to the very effective power exerted by Theodoric.

The change in the status of Gaul in the last years of the century was even more dramatic than the changes in Italy. The Gallic change first appeared in the north of the former diocese. At a time nearly 40 years before Theodoric's reign started, the region of northern Gaul experienced a period of relative stability. As outlined earlier, this was initiated by Aegidius, the commander-in-chief who had declared his independence and taken control of the region in 457. When Aegidius died in 464, stability continued under his successor, his son Syagrius, until the death of Childeric, the King of the Franks, in 481.

Childeric, whose western borders adjoined the Kingdom of Soissons, as Aegidius's territory was named, had formed an alliance of mutual respect with the *magister militum* which continued unchanged under Syagrius. The latter, however, had neither the power nor the authority of his father. He never held his father's military rank and, as a result, never had the unquestioning confidence and obedience of his troops, nor had he the Roman military experience which a military career would have given. An additional problem for Syagrius was the presence in his kingdom of large numbers of *Bagaudae* (groups of disaffected peasants similar to those who had confronted Maximian two centuries earlier), who had banded together against Roman injustice and oppression. All these factors were to have decisive consequences for the future of Syagrius and of Gaul. The results are fully set out in Gregory of Tours's book, *The History of the Franks*.

As previously explained, the largest body of information on late fifth-century history of northern Gaul comes from Bishop Gregory's book, written only some 50 years after the work by Gildas. The two men's approaches to history could hardly be more different. Gildas has a point to make – to attribute the ills suffered by Britain to a fall from grace of its rulers. The information Gregory supplies on the rulers of northern Gaul shows them to be as depraved as those in Britain, whose deeds were described by Gildas. Gregory records the most violent and cruel acts in a matter-of-fact way, accepting them without criticism, and yet, in other places, a strong feeling for justice and compassion becomes very apparent. He was a man of his time but his character, as displayed by his writing, gives confidence in the validity of the information he provides.

Childeric was succeeded by his son Clovis, who had no intention of continuing the alliance between the Franks and the Kingdom of Soissons. In consequence, Syagrius no longer had a friend on his eastern border but was faced by a Germanic tribe which was as antagonistic as were the German tribes facing Ambrosius in Britain. Hence at the start of the 480s, after Romulus had been deposed by Odoacer, there were still two western defenders of the Roman tradition, Syagrius in Gaul and Ambrosius in Britain, but after the death of Aegidius both were now facing aggressive enemies on their eastern borders. The determined opposition by Vortimer and Ambrosius has been described in the previous chapter. The opposition presented by Syagrius was something different.

Clovis was only 16 when his father died but he soon showed his exceptional military and political skills. He died a comparatively young man at the age of 45, but during the 30 years of his active life he changed the face of Gaul and set the pattern for the development of France. His first action after accession was to make his own kingdom supreme over all the other petty Frankish kingdoms and this he did ruthlessly in the first few years of his reign. He then turned his attention to Syagrius and the Kingdom of Soissons on his western flank.

As indicated earlier, the position held by Syagrius within his own kingdom was by no means as secure as that held by his father, Aegidius. Consequent upon his military weakness and the activity of the *Bagaudae*, his writ did not extend far beyond the city of Soissons.

Roman authority, unaided by imperial support from Italy, was becoming increasingly unacceptable to the Gallic population of his small kingdom.

Nevertheless, when Clovis challenged Syagrius to defend his kingdom, the latter did not hesitate to respond. In the event, Clovis met Syagrius at some unknown site not far from Soissons in 486 and had no difficulty in inflicting total defeat. The engagement was relatively minor, probably involving less than 3,000 troops on either side, but it was important as it defined the start of a military campaign by Clovis which was to have profound consequences for the development of Gaul. After the battle Syagrius fled south to the neighbouring Kingdom of the Visigoths, where he sought shelter with Alaric II, their king, who ruled from Toulouse. With single-minded directness, Clovis demanded that the defeated Roman should be handed over under the threat of war if Alaric did not comply. With a weaker character than Clovis, Alaric submitted to the threat and returned Syagrius to Clovis, who, with typical ruthlessness, put him to death.

The residual Gallo-Roman forces in Soissons immediately transferred their allegiance from Syagrius to Clovis and they, together with the land and wealth of Soissons, formed the basis of Clovis's growing prosperity. His frontiers now rested on the Loire and the city of Soissons became his capital. The whole of the Channel coast of Gaul, only excluding Brittany, was now under the control of the Franks.

The defeat of Syagrius had serious consequences for Ambrosius, also facing Germanic tribes in Britain, and for his successor, Arthur. Apart from the Celtic inhabitants of Brittany, who remained outside the realms of Clovis and his descendants, the Romano-Celtic rulers of Britain could no longer rely on friendly Romano-Celts on the other side of the Channel. As a consequence, the rulers of Britain were effectively isolated from the successor states in southern Gaul and Italy, and even further from any influence of the eastern Roman Empire.

Clovis had no intention of limiting his penetration of Gaul to his new southern boundary, the River Loire. After a pause of five years he made a foray in 491 against the Thuringians, a tribe on the eastern boundary of the Frankish lands. Here he was unsuccessful. His next move was in the diplomatic rather than the military sphere. He no doubt had some expectation of including the Burgundians, who had settled around the headwaters of the Rhône, within his kingdom. To further this ambition, in about 493 he married Clotilda, a Catholic Christian and the niece of Gundobad of the royal house of the Burgundians – a sound political move, the consequences of which helped Clovis on many future occasions.

Some years later, possibly in 496, Clovis decided to attack the Alemanni. This Germanic tribe lay to the south of the Frankish lands round the mouth of the Rhine and to the east of the recently conquered Kingdom of Soissons. The south-western borders of the Alemanni faced the Burgundian lands on the upper Rhône. The Alemanni were defeated, but the site of the battle is not known with certainty. There is a legend that Clovis's victory at a critical point in the engagement was the result of a bargain he made with God to abandon his pagan beliefs in favour of the Catholic faith should he defeat the Alemanni. After his victory he was certainly baptized into the Christian faith as a Catholic, but the story of the bargain with God is far more likely to be an instance where Clovis took advantage of the credulity of his subjects in order to explain a change in his religious affiliations. It is much more probable that he adopted his wife's faith in order to gain the support of all the Catholic bishops of Gaul, who were the dominant power in the Gallic cities, exerting far more influence there than their civil counterparts.

There is also another reason why Clovis chose the Catholic faith. It so happened that many of the German tribes had already been converted to Christianity by Arian missionaries, whose belief was that Christ was in some measure inferior to God the Father. This belief was anathema to the Catholic hierarchy and Clovis, from the time of his conversion, had the moral encouragement of both the bishops and the Catholic Gallo-Roman population in any attack he made on German tribes holding Arian beliefs.

In addition, Clovis's conversion endeared him to Bishop Gregory of Tours, but fortunately not to the extent of persuading Gregory to suppress any information relating to the ruthless behaviour of the Frankish king. He merely excused Clovis on the grounds that he was doing God's will in destroying the heretical opposition to the Catholic Church.

The defeat of the Alemanni placed Clovis on the northern border of the Burgundians, another mainly Arian German tribe (despite the fact that Clotilda was a Catholic). Clovis again moved to attack in the year 500. The Burgundians had settled round the headwaters of the Rhône and on the Saône, and were ruled by two brothers, Gundobad (Clotilda's uncle) and Godigisel. Battle was joined when the two brothers met Clovis near Dijon. The ensuing engagement ended quickly in favour of the Franks when Godigisel betrayed his brother and led his troops over to Clovis. Gundobad fled south to Avignon, where he was followed and besieged. However, with a line of communications and supply well over 320 kilometres (200 miles) in length, Clovis was over-extended and was forced to withdraw back to his frontiers, leaving Gundobad undefeated in Avignon. After Clovis's retreat, Gundobad regained control of the Burgundian lands when he defeated and killed Godigisel at Vienne.

Clovis made use of the Burgundian reverse to regroup his forces and it is possible that, at this stage of his campaigns, his military strength now lay chiefly in the Gallo-Roman soldiers he had recruited in Soissons and elsewhere subsequent to his Catholic conversion. His generals were almost certainly Franks, but Frankish other ranks were probably outnumbered by Gallo-Romans.

After the regrouping, and with his appetite for conquest still unsatiated, Clovis turned his attention to the south-east. He knew that across his Loire frontier he faced another Arian German tribe, the Visigoths, led by Alaric II. He also knew that, once again, action in this direction would gain the support of his Catholic subjects, and furthermore, he had already assessed Alaric's weakness of character, as demonstrated by the surrender of Syagrius under Clovis's threat of war.

There were, however, other less favourable considerations. It was very possible that the Visigoths would be supported by their compatriots, the Ostrogoths, and their leader, Theodoric, King of Italy, but to balance this negative factor, some restraint might be exercised on Theodoric by the Emperor Anastasius in Constantinople. The latter, resenting the usurpation of the throne of the western empire by Theodoric, would probably support any action, such as Clovis's offensive against the Visigoths, which could contain Theodoric's growing sphere of influence. A threat from the east might deter Theodoric from moving west to help the Visigoths. A final factor in Clovis's calculations was the knowledge that the Burgundians had always maintained a close accord with Constantinople. With all these considerations in mind, Clovis decided to offer the hand of friendship to Gundobad and to establish an alliance with the Burgundians.

Indications of Frankish warlike intentions directed against Alaric were very apparent to Theodoric, who decided to intervene. His first attempt was on the diplomatic front. He wrote to all the parties concerned, Clovis, Alaric and Gundobad, together with some Germanic kingdoms bordering Clovis, asking all either to show restraint or to use their good offices in support of peace. He also sent ambassadors to the Visigoths, the Franks and the Burgundians to emphasize his views.

All these attempts to maintain peace were of no avail and in 507 Clovis left his new capital, Paris, and marched against Alaric. After crossing the Loire, battle was joined at Vouillé, near Poitiers. Alaric was killed and the Visigoths decisively beaten. They retreated from Toulouse and from Gaul into Spain. All trace of the Arian heresy was eliminated from Aquitaine, and Clovis's frontier now rested on the Pyrenees. His victory was aided by an attack made by the Burgundians on the eastern flank of the Visigoths, and for this they were rewarded by the gift of Provence, bringing their frontier to the Mediterranean. To substantiate the gift, the combined armies of Franks and Burgundians advanced on Arles and laid siege to the town.

His efforts at peacemaking having failed, Theodoric decided on active intervention. He was, however, facing danger on two fronts. The fleet of the eastern emperor was attacking the heel of Italy in an attempt to distract Theodoric from any westward adventures, and Clovis was dangerously close to the north-western border of Italy. The Ostrogoth king, with supreme confidence in his own abilities, therefore resolved to divide his forces into two parts and attack both adversaries at the same time. He was successful on both fronts. His generals marched through Provence and relieved Arles and, at the same time, his other army cleared southern Italy of Anastasius's forces.

Theodoric imposed a peace settlement on Clovis and in it the region of Septimania, roughly coinciding with Languedoc, was restored to the Visigoths, giving them back a small part of their kingdom north of the Pyrenees. For his own reward, Theodoric took Provence, ejecting the Burgundians northwards from territory they had only just occupied after the victory of Vouillé.

Shortly after this last campaign, in the year 511, Clovis died in Paris. In the short space of 30 years he had extended his territories from a petty kingdom on the Rhine to almost the whole of Gaul. Only Brittany, Septimania, Provence and the Burgundian kingdom on the Rhône remained outside his control. He certainly laid the foundations of the medieval nation state of France, but the important consequence for the present argument lies in the new directions taken by the growing nation as a result of the achievements of this exceptional man.

Such was the speed of the Frankish conquest that many parts of Gaul were unaffected by the invaders' campaigns. A high proportion of the wealthier houses and farms were not disturbed and remained in the hands of their previous owners, who were, of course, Gallo-Romans. Indeed, after the conquest it is probable that the Franks comprised not more than 10 per cent of the total population. Because these barbarian invaders were led by a ruler who had his own system of absolute power, the native inhabitants were merely exchanging one autocrat for another; the Roman system in the late fifth century was both autocratic and corrupt.

Under the new dispensation, the Franks, although relatively few in number, were at the top of the social pyramid. The Frankish commanders, often counts, were given charge of districts with both civil and military authority. These men owed their allegiance to Clovis, who, as a German king, was an absolute ruler with the whole realm his personal property. Nevertheless, wealthy and powerful Gallo-Romans soon rose to the higher levels of the new society as the reality of social order prevailed.

The two chief components of the new nation, the Gallo-Romans and the Franks, commenced a process of integration which involved changes in the social order of both. Two of the most notable changes concerned the realms of language and the law. The languages of the western Roman Empire and the surrounding barbarian nations all formed part of the Indo-European family of languages, which originated in India and spread through Iran and Russia to Europe. Three groups of this family penetrated to western Europe: the Teutonic group, spoken by the Franks, by the various tribes which invaded Britain and by the other Germanic tribes which invaded Gaul; the Celtic group, spoken by the native inhabitants of Britain, Ireland, Spain and Gaul; and the Romance group, of which Latin is a member, spoken by the Roman conquerors of Britain, Spain and Gaul.

In the new kingdom of Clovis, at the start of his reign the court, the military leaders and the administrators spoke a Teutonic language akin to the languages spoken by the invaders of Britain. The Gallo-Romans, who had long abandoned the Celtic language of pre-Roman Gaul, now spoke Latin. This language was not, however, the classical language of ancient Rome but rather the Vulgar Latin spoken by the western Roman Empire. Over the next century, the two languages were used side by side, but gradually use of the Frankish language declined and the speech of the Gallo-Romans predominated, slowly developing from Vulgar Latin through Old French and Middle French into the modern French language, one of the four major modern languages derived from the classical Latin of the early Roman Empire. Modern French owes only about 10 per cent of its vocabulary to the language of the Franks who conquered Gaul in the early years of the sixth century.

Diverting from the main theme for a moment, it is interesting to recall that a very similar language situation developed in England after the Norman Conquest in 1066. As in the case of the Franks, the

Normans imposed their language, French, in the court, in high administration and in military matters, leaving English as the language of the native population in local affairs, in agriculture and in trade. In a few centuries, just as in Gaul, the invaders' language declined and the use of English spread to all classes of society and gradually developed from its Anglo-Saxon origins to the modern English spoken today.

The progress of Gallo-Roman and Frankish integration involved another important facet of society: the legal system. Before the conquest, the Frankish system was based on the Lex Salica or Salic Law, of which the main feature was a very detailed table of compensations to be paid for all personal injuries from minor wounds to death. Similar tables applied to compensations for theft. These arrangements were designed to eliminate the danger of development of blood feuds between families. The Gallo-Romans, on the other hand, were subject to the far more comprehensive Roman Law, which was particularly detailed in the fields of trade and industry.

The barbarian conquerors of Gaul, the Visigoths and Burgundians, as well as Franks, did not, however, wish to destroy any Roman institution which they admired or could adapt to their own purposes, and one such institution was the Roman legal system. The Franks in particular favoured a personalized law – that is to say, they were prepared to allow the people they conquered to be judged under their own systems of law. Consequently, the two legal systems, the Salic and the Roman, existed side by side in the early years after the conquest. The Roman Law, however, applied to by far the larger part of the population.

As time passed, it became necessary to write down the many clauses of the Salic Law in the universal written language of the time, Latin. This task could be done only by men who were well acquainted with Roman Law and it is certain they introduced aspects of the latter into the Salic code. As the inhabitants of the country became conscious of their nationhood, it became essential to adopt a territorial legal system where all the inhabitants of the nation were subject to the same law. In the end, Roman Law became the main source for the legal systems of France and Continental Europe for five reasons. First, because the Franks and the other invading barbarians of Gaul, Italy and Spain did not eliminate the Roman legal system; second, because the growing nation states favoured a territorial law; third, because Roman Law was more compatible with the growth of trade and industry; fourth, because Roman Law was familiar to the greater part of the population; and, finally, because the codified law was written in Latin.

In summary, the last quasi-Roman enclave in northern Gaul was quickly conquered by Clovis, who, after destroying Syagrius, employed the Roman troops of the Kingdom of Soissons alongside his own Frankish warriors to extend his conquests to most of the rest of Gaul. The new nation was formed by an amalgam of Gallo-Romans, Franks, Visigoths and other peoples. It adopted Vulgar Latin as a language rather than the Teutonic dialects of the invaders and strong elements of Roman Law appeared in the Salic Law used by the Franks. A decisive step in the growth of the new Frankish kingdom was the conversion of Clovis to the Catholic faith in 496, and in the course of the next 300 years there was a revival of a new Roman Empire in the west.

In the year 800 the Frankish King Charles the Great, Charlemagne, was crowned emperor by Pope Leo III on Christmas Day in St Peter's Church in Rome. After three centuries the Celtic, Roman, German and Christian elements in western Europe were united in a new empire of the west which, however, excluded England, Scotland, Wales and Ireland, together with Spain (much of which had been conquered by Islam). Although this new empire lasted only about a century, it represented an outcome very different from that taking place in the other western Roman diocese, Britain.

# Conquest and Post-conquest in Britain

THE MARKED change in direction from a decaying Roman province in northern Gaul to a Frankish kingdom covering most of Gaul started in the early days of Clovis's campaigns and ended after the 30 years of his military campaigns. The pattern for the future of France was firmly set in those 30 years on the basis of the amalgam of Frankish, Gallo-Roman and other barbarian tribes resulting from the success of Clovis's campaigns. The first phase of the conquest of Britain, described in Chapter 4, initiated changes in the course of British history north of the Channel. The later phases added to these changes and introduced the post-conquest development of English history into the former Roman diocese.

The overall duration of the conquest, the time taken for the pattern of a future England to evolve, was very much longer than the 30 years it took Clovis to establish in Gaul his concept of the future pattern for France. Although the Anglo-Saxon invaders of Britain were as Germanic in origin as were the Franks, and although in the end they were as successful as the Franks, it took about 150 years for them to subdue most of Britain south of the Humber, compared with the 30 years of the Frankish conflict. Possible reasons for this difference in timescale will be examined first and after that the successive phases of the long campaign in Britain will be considered in more detail.

The causes for the long campaign in Britain and the comparatively short campaign in Gaul must chiefly be ascribed to differences in the resistance of the invaded peoples and in the aggression of the invaders. There is, however, one factor outside these two primary causes which first has to be eliminated. It might be argued that the logistical problems of supply and reinforcements faced by the Franks were simpler than those faced by the Anglo-Saxons. The former certainly were opposed only by river barriers while crossing the plains of northern France, whereas the latter were faced with a difficult North Sea crossing.

The strength of this argument is, however, diminished by archaeological discoveries in East Anglia. The absence of fifth-century inhumation sites in Norfolk, favoured by the Romano-British, and the presence of large early fifth-century cremation cemeteries, favoured by the Angles, indicate occupation by the invaders from the start of the century and no reoccupation by the British at any subsequent time. The logistical problems in East Anglia were thus solved, for, from the early fifth century onwards, the Angles always had bases for withdrawal, reinforcements and supply. In addition, documentary evidence from Gildas and Nennius shows that, by the fourth decade of the fifth century, the invaders also had a secure base in Kent. According to *The Anglo-Saxon Chronicle,* secure Saxon bases were also established along the south coast before the end of the fifth century. Supply bases were thus available for all the invading tribes by the turn of the century.

In any case, the logistical problems were not severe. Engagements between opposing forces in those times usually involved no more than 1,000 troops on each side, and such numbers were small enough to be fed by raids on the surrounding countryside. All these considerations make it difficult to ascribe the difference in campaign length to logistical problems faced by the Anglo-Saxons.

Returning, then, to differences between invaders and defenders, it is necessary to examine the qualities of four groups: the Franks and the Anglo-Saxons, on the one hand, and the Gallo-Romans and the Romano-British, on the other. In the first place, it is unlikely that differences in the military abilities of the Anglo-Saxons and the Franks were a cause of the disparity in the campaign durations, for such differences were minimal. The Anglo-Saxons and the Franks were neighbouring Germanic tribes, with similar military equipment and fighting spirit. The Franks had their *francisca,* a single-edged throwing axe, and the Saxons their *saxa* or short sword, but their shield, spear and other gear were very similar. There is a record of aggressive behaviour common to all the Germanic tribes of north-western Europe. Contemporary historians claimed that war was the ordinary avocation of the Franks, and no reader of *Beowulf* could ever doubt that any tribes to the north of the Franks were at least as aggressive.

It would be equally difficult to contend that the military abilities of the native troops in Britain and Gaul who faced the invaders were in any major respect dissimilar. Both would have inherited to some degree the military expertise of the Romans, as well as the courage and prowess of the Celts. Both had, in fact, repelled the barbarian invasions around 410 without the assistance of Rome. Aegidius was a *magister militum* and no doubt organized his troops efficiently and maintained their morale. Clovis certainly appreciated their excellence and incorporated them into his army for later campaigns. In Britain, Vortigern and Vortimer had used Romano-British troops to push back the early incursions of the invaders after their first thrust westwards, a process ending with the three Kentish battles of 455 to 465 (see Map 1 on page 64). After 470 Ambrosius, with his recruitment centres, had used similar troops to keep the invaders within their coastal bridgeheads (see Map 2 on page 71). The British and Gallic troops had very similar backgrounds and expertise. Clearly, in Britain, as well as in Gaul, the native forces were no mean opponents for the invading barbarians.

It is, then, possible to eliminate both logistics and the military spirit, gear and abilities of both aggressors and defenders as causes for the difference in campaign length. This leaves organization and control of the military forces as the remaining possible causes, and here contrasts can be found.

In Gaul, Clovis attacked and defeated his opponents one by one, piecemeal, and in each case his advances were swift and decisive. After gaining control of all the Frankish tribes soon after his father's death, he defeated Syagrius in 486, the Alemanni in 496 and Alaric II in 507, with consolidation in between. There were some reverses: he was less than successful against the Thuringians in 491 and against the Burgundians in 500. Nevertheless, after each reverse he regrouped and came back to the attack.

In Britain, the invasion was also piecemeal but the separate invasion campaigns were led by different leaders. The first wave was led by Hengist (although the East Anglian invasion may have occurred even earlier, there are no records of any individual leader), the second by Aelle and the third by Cerdic. Here, however, it was the defenders, first under the leadership of Vortigern and Vortimer and later under Ambrosius and his successor, rather than the aggressors who displayed a consistent and successful response. Hengist's campaigns were protracted, extending over the period 446–65, and involved both advances and retreats. The same lack of clear and decisive success will be seen later in this chapter to apply to both Aelle and Cerdic.

From the middle of the fifth century to the first decades of the sixth, the indifferent success of the Anglo-Saxons is in strong contrast to the overall success of the Franks in Gaul. In addition, the success of the British leaders, who by 520 had still restricted the invaders to East Anglia, Kent and a narrow strip of the south coast, is in equal sharp contrast with the successive failures of Syagrius, the leaders of the Alemanni and Alaric II to restrain the swift advances of Clovis southwards.

The differences in leadership do indicate that this factor played a dominant role in determining the duration of the barbarian conquests of Britain and Gaul. It is possible that Clovis's military efficiency made a relatively short campaign possible in Gaul and that the abilities of the British leaders in the years between 455 and 520 made the corresponding campaign in Britain much longer.

The consistent and often successful British leadership is in marked contrast with the failure of both Gallo-Roman and Visigoth leadership on the other side of the Channel, and detailed evidence for this superiority of the British leaders can be found in Gildas, Nennius and *The Anglo-Saxon Chronicle*. These sources, at the same time, provide the supporting evidence for the length of the campaign. As will be seen, it is particularly useful if the *Chronicle* can be used to confirm British successes, because it mentions neither Ambrosius nor Arthur by name and is naturally biased against the British and in favour of the invaders.

This influence of leadership can most usefully be shown by considering separately the various component parts of the whole invasion campaign in Britain between 446 and 597, and some six parts or phases can be distinguished (see Appendix 3). The first of these was described in Chapter 4 (see Map 1 on page 64) and included the major drive to the west by Hengist, so vividly reported by Gildas, and the subsequent British recovery. This revival, the first stage of a two-part process, was initiated by Vortigern and completed by his son Vortimer.

This stage of the recovery process ended in the third of the three Kentish battles. It has already been mentioned in Chapter 4 that the British and the invaders both claimed victory in these engagements but that the *Chronicle* account fits well with the concept of a British revival overreaching itself. There is further evidence in support of this conclusion in the Nennius record.

The victory claim in Nennius for the three battles is preceded by a paragraph (Chapter 43) which states that 'Vortimer fought vigorously against Hengist and Horsa and their people, and expelled them as far as the aforesaid island called Thanet, and there three times shut them up and besieged them'. The record of the three battles, in one of which 'there fell Horsa', is placed in the following paragraph and consequently took place after the Thanet siege. It is not possible for any of the battles to be located east of Thanet and so these three battles must be located to the west of Thanet. This must confirm again, even from the British record, that Vortimer's drive to the east as far as Thanet had resulted in a loss of initiative and was followed by battles to the west of Thanet where Hengist reconsolidated his hold on the south bank of the Thames.

The archaeological evidence from the cemeteries also supports the *Chronicle* viewpoint. Of the early fifth-century invaders of Britain, the Jutes preferred inhumation and the Angles, together with the Saxons, cremation. The cemeteries south of the Thames in this period favour inhumation and so confirm the *Chronicle* indication that Jutes were living here at that time, and, very reasonably, were consolidating their hold on the region. Although the Romano-British also favoured inhumation, Gildas also confirms that the Saxons 'fixed their dreadful claws on the east side of the island' before the great raid in the 440s and he never reports any British reconquest of Kent. All of these arguments indicate that the *Chronicle* view of the conclusion to this first stage of British recovery is more probable than the record in Nennius.

However, in spite of Hengist's victories in Kent, the invaders had in fact been forced back into their original bridgehead. About 20 years had elapsed between the first aggressive drive of the Saxon forces to the west (440–46) and the three Kentish battles (455–65) which indicated a return of the invaders to their first landing sites. Two-thirds of the length of Clovis's whole campaign, 20 years, had been spent, with effectively little success for the invaders apart from the fact that they had not been expelled from Britain. This achievement was a notable success for British leadership, unfortunately somewhat dimmed both by the victories of the invaders in their first surge westwards and also by the victories gained by Hengist at the end of the period. At this point of the overall campaign, the leadership honours were fairly evenly divided between the invaders and the British.

The end of the first stage of British recovery is also marked by the end of Hengist's active participation in the conquest of Britain. The *Chronicle* reports only one further victory for him, in 473, but provides no information on the place of the battle. After that his name disappears from the records, and so does any evidence of further progress of the invaders in the south-east until Aethelbert's reign in the later years of the sixth century. Hengist's son Aesc succeeded to the kingdom (of Kent) in 488 and this year presumably marked the death of

Hengist. There is thus an indication that Hengist did, at the end of his life, spend some 15 years, from 473 to 488, in comparative retirement from any active military commitments. He was probably a contemporary of Vortigern, having first landed in Britain in 428, some three years after Vortigern's accession in 425. Thus, like Vortigern, he may have been in his sixties at the time of the Kent battles and almost certainly would have retired from active service after 473.

By the same token, the retirement and death of Vortigern must also have occurred not too long after the Kentish battles and the death of his most able son, Vortimer. As suggested earlier, his reputation would probably have been discredited by the consequences of the great raid and additionally by Hengist's reoccupation of Kent after the largely successful British recovery. For these reasons the popularity and prestige of Vortigern's party had probably declined.

Conversely, the authority of the party once led by the Elder Ambrosius, and now led by Ambrosius Aurelianus, must have increased. This viewpoint is supported by the reference in Nennius (Chapter 48) to the Younger Ambrosius as 'the great king among all the kings of the British nation' who gave permission for Pascent, one of Vortigern's sons, to rule in two 'countries', Builth and Gwerthrynion. The accession of Ambrosius can probably be dated to around 470 and under his leadership the second stage of the British recovery commenced. This recovery saw the end of the first phase of the conquest in 477.

The second stage of British recovery, which started with the accession of Ambrosius as High King, continued over into the second phase of the conquest. This phase deals with further efforts made by the new British leader to limit the advances of the invaders, if not to eject them from the island. There are no specific records of victories gained by Ambrosius in battle, apart from the comment by Gildas: 'Under him our people regained their strength, and challenged the victors to battle. The Lord assented and the battle went their way. From then on victory went now to our countrymen, now to their enemies.' These victories, however, ensured a fairly stable position in Britain south of the Humber in the third quarter of the fifth century and were a consequence of the action taken by Ambrosius. Lincolnshire, Norfolk and Suffolk were held by Angles and Kent remained in the hands of Aesc, Hengist's son. The centre, south and west of Britain was controlled by Ambrosius, the new High King.

In spite of the lack of direct evidence of second-phase Ambrosian victories in either Nennius or Gildas, there is some evidence of specific success which can be deduced from two entries in *The Anglo-Saxon Chronicle* for the years 477 and 490. These entries can be related to the recruitment sites Ambrosius set up in the years following his accession and described in Chapter 4. The location of some of these sites (see Map 2 on page 71) to the north-east of London and along the south coast indicates that Ambrosius had made dispositions for the protection of Britain from either actual or potential invaders. The line of recruitment sites for Ambrosius's troops between London and Colchester was clearly an attempt to protect London from further penetration southwards out of the bridgeheads in Norfolk and Suffolk. It will be argued in Chapter 8 that the sites to the north of London played a useful part in restraining the Angles until the second decade of the sixth century and in discouraging them for several decades after that. It is, however, the sites near the south coast that are of concern here and could well be related to the second phase of the invasion sequence, to be considered next.

This phase of the conquest was initiated in 477, at a time when Ambrosius was completing the second stage of British recovery. As briefly mentioned earlier, the *Chronicle* reports that a leader of the Saxons named Aelle made a successful landing near Selsey in 477 – the earliest invasion activity on the south coast. After some fighting at places not clearly identified, he moved along the coast eastwards and took the town of Andred near Pevensey in 490 (see Map 2 on page 71). In a period of 13 years, Aelle's South Saxon forces had not apparently subdued any inland areas and, in addition, Aelle's name is never mentioned again after 490.

The very limited success of the invaders revealed in the second phase of the overall campaign is some measure of the high quality of the military dispositions planned by Ambrosius, for it is very possible that the Ambrosian recruitment sites on the south coast between Selsey and Pevensey played no small part in the restriction of Aelle to areas close to the coast. However, in spite of this very modest achievement, according to Bede (Chapter 5, Book 2), Aelle was regarded in later centuries as a man of greater importance than simply the leader of the South Saxons. A possible reason for this will be suggested in the next chapter.

At the conclusion of the first two phases of the conquest, it is clear that the invaders had made little progress beyond their bridgeheads in East Anglia and Kent. At the same time, there is a difference in the assessment of the two phases which has to be emphasized. For the first phase, which stretched from 440 to 477, it is possible to examine and correlate British and Anglo-Saxon sources. For the second phase, from 477 to 490, British action has to be deduced from Dr Morris's research, supplemented by limited information from Gildas.

Correlation between the *Chronicle* and British sources for this phase (and for most of the later phases) has usually to be inferred, for it is in fact rarely provided. Much of the lack of close correlation may be attributed to the natural wish of the recorders, whoever they might have been, to record victories gained by their side but conveniently to forget defeats. Consequently, a deficient record provided by the invaders or the defenders may conceal a decisive advantage gained by their opponents. There are also gaps in the records on both sides and these may be due either to the recorders' lack of information or to a pause in the invasion process. In the latter case, particularly if the gap occurs in the *Chronicle*, which provides a fuller sequence of dated events, the cause could be attributed to firmer opposition from the defenders. Their victories would be glossed over without even recording the engagement.

The third and very critical phase of the invasion sequence started at a time roughly coincident with the end of Aelle's South Saxon campaign and ended in the second decade of the sixth century. This time the chief information source is Nennius, with supplementary evidence from Gildas, *The Anglo-Saxon Chronicle* and the *Annales Cambriae*. During this phase British superiority over the invaders is described throughout a period in which the *Chronicle* records only coastal activity on the part of the invaders. As will be described later, in the three decades of this phase, from 490 to 517, only one clear Anglo-Saxon victory is claimed by the *Chronicle*. This happened in 508 at Netley, near Southampton Water. There were two other landings, at Portsmouth and an unknown site at 'Cerdic's-ore' during the same period, but no record of advances inland from the coast.

At the start of the third phase, the British struggle against the invaders was probably still being led by Ambrosius, who, by the mid-480s, must have been approaching 60 years of age. In order for the struggle against the invaders to continue, another leader must have been ready to take Ambrosius's place, at least as the active military leader in the field. This could be no other than Arthur.

It is difficult to accept that Ambrosius, whose importance is vouched for by Gildas, was responsible for all the major actions against the invaders, even if the age limitation is disregarded. Such acceptance would give no reason for the bards to sing the praises of any leader other than Ambrosius. The fame of Ambrosius in both Gildas and Nennius, in conjunction with the praise of Arthur in Nennius and by the bards, compels acceptance of the latter's existence, and this conclusion is also supported by references to Arthur in the *Annales Cambriae*.

Although it is quite possible that Ambrosius was still the High King at the start of the third phase, there is evidence in Nennius that Arthur was the military leader of the British, perhaps the commander-in-chief of the ageing High King. In the early years of this phase a list of 12 battles is provided in Nennius and it is reported that 'he [Arthur] was victorious in all his campaigns'. A sequence of 12 victories might well be advanced as evidence for Arthur as a brilliantly successful military leader, but doubts arise on the nature of the evidence. The last battle was at Badon Hill, the only one for which Gildas gives supporting evidence, but he does not, unfortunately, state explicitly the name of the British leader at Badon. He does give a firm date for this last battle, placing it in the year of his birth, which can be calculated to fall in the last few years of the fifth century, probably about 496 (this date is preferred to the *Annales Cambriae* date of 516; a date of 517 for the battle of Camlann is preferred to the *Annales Cambriae* date of 537, thus keeping a gap of 21 years between Badon and Arthur's death). None of the other 11 battles in Nennius is dated and it is probable that the whole list is taken from a bardic poem, and poetic evidence standing alone is of doubtful value. These factors make it difficult at this stage of the argument to use Nennius, without corroboration, to support Arthur's military genius. Nevertheless, Nennius considered the prose battle list sufficiently important to include in his book.

Equally, the report of the 12 battles cannot do much in itself to confirm the overall campaign length when the date of the last battle at Badon Hill is firmly dated around the turn of the century, some 90 years before the conquest of Britain was completed. At the time of Badon, Clovis was about to attack the Alemanni and was within 13 years of ending his conquest of Gaul.

As a result, neither the list of the victories nor their effect on the overall length of the conquest can be accorded much weight, at this point, in establishing either the reputation or importance of Arthur. Consequently, it is not proposed to say anything more on the third phase in this chapter. The phase will be reconsidered later, when the length of the conquest and the contrast with Gaul are proved. The fourth and subsequent phases of the conquest will therefore be considered next, followed by a survey of the direction taken by the Anglo-Saxons after their conquest was successfully completed at the end of the sixth century.

However, before moving on to the fourth phase of the conquest, it is important to mention the East Anglian situation. By the start of the sixth century, the *Chronicle* has still made no reference to events in East Anglia. The invaders of this part of Britain, possibly the earliest of all, do not appear in the records until the third quarter of the sixth century. It has, however, already been noted that evidence from the cemeteries suggests occupation of East Anglia by the Angles in the early fifth century. Other archaeological evidence suggests permanent exclusion of the Romano-British inhabitants thereafter.

In so far as numbers of Angles are concerned, Procopius reports that early in the sixth century the Continental home of the Angles was empty, and Bede writes that this area was still unpopulated in the eighth century. Clearly a substantial bridgehead existed in East Anglia in the first half of the fifth century, but there is no indication that these invaders made any major outward expansion into central Britain south of the Humber until late in the sixth century.

Cemetery evidence suggests a minor incursion of the invaders into the region of the upper Thames near Oxford and they may have come south from East Anglia via the Icknield Way or, alternatively, up the Thames valley. No victories or military leaders in this area are, however, recorded around the turn of the century. Nevertheless, the question of East Anglian expansion is vital to any understanding of the third and fifth phases of the conquest and will resurface when these are considered.

After Aelle's last engagement in 490, the *Chronicle*'s attention changes again and is directed to the fourth phase, the invasion of the West Saxons. The initial years of this phase overlap the third-phase records of British activities (see Appendix 3). Despite this overlap, records of British victories in the third phase are entirely missing from the *Chronicle*, as equally are West Saxon victories from Nennius. Nevertheless, a relationship between the Nennius and *Chronicle* records can be found and, as will be seen later, this relationship goes some way to confirm the veracity of both.

At the start of the fourth phase, the *Chronicle* records the landing of the West Saxons and names their first leaders in Britain as Cerdic and his son Cynric (although the relationship between Cerdic and Cynric is questionable). They arrived in 495, probably near Southampton; the date coincides closely with the date of the British victory at Badon. The nationality of Cerdic is uncertain, for the name itself is British rather than Saxon, and it is quite possible that Cerdic was a British leader who joined forces with the invaders and fought with them against his own countrymen. This characteristic lack of racial loyalty among Celtic leaders was a factor which assisted Caesar in his conquest of both Britain and Gaul, as was noted in Chapter 2.

The landing was opposed at first for, as we are told, an engagement with the British took place on the day of the landing but no victory was claimed by the West Saxons. In some way perhaps an agreement was reached between the British and the invaders which ended in an integration between Cerdic and his people and the West Saxons (archaeological DNA research published in 1996 supports some British–Saxon integration). This Saxon tribe became one of the most important to invade Britain and Bede recognized their worth. He provided a list of Anglo-Saxon Bretwaldas (a title roughly equivalent to the British High King) south of the Humber (Chapter 5, Book 2). According to Bede, the first Bretwalda was Aelle, the leader of the South Saxons (despite his limited success). The second was Ceawlin of the West Saxons, the great-grandson of Cerdic; the third was Aethelbert of Kent and the fourth Raedwald of the East Angles.

In 508, 13 years after the landing, Cerdic led the West Saxons against a loyal British king named Natanleod and defeated him (see Map 3 on page 94). The defeated king is remembered to this day in the name of the town Netley Marsh, at the head of Southampton Water. In the campaign that ensued, Cerdic and his successors followed a logical sequence. They were attempting to carve out a kingdom in that part of Britain falling outside the spheres of influence of the South Saxons or of the Angles and Jutes. Their plan, based on the evidence of their movements taken from the *Chronicle*, could have been to secure the Isle of Wight and to cut the two main Roman roads from Salisbury and Bath to London, so isolating the British in the south-west from their compatriots in the centre of the island.

It has to be recognized that the dates given in the *Chronicle* for the West Saxon campaign may not be absolutely accurate, but they do fall into a sequence which is in accord with the geographical location of the battles as shown in Map 3. This campaign also fits naturally in the time following after Aelle's campaign and, as will be seen later, precedes the Anglian campaign in the third quarter of the sixth century.

After the victory at Netley in 508, Cerdic's westward advance took him in 519 to the second battle, located at Charford, 14 kilometres (nine miles) west of Netley. Although the *Chronicle* records that date as the start of the West Saxon dynasty, it does not specifically claim a victory at Charford. A third battle at an unidentified site, 'Cerdic's-ley', is also recorded, in 527, again without a victory claim.

The lack of claimed victories at Charford and 'Cerdic's-ley' may have been the cause of a halt to further advance inland, for the *Chronicle* records a fall back to the coast in order to attack and take the Isle of Wight in 530. After this conquest there was a change in leadership of

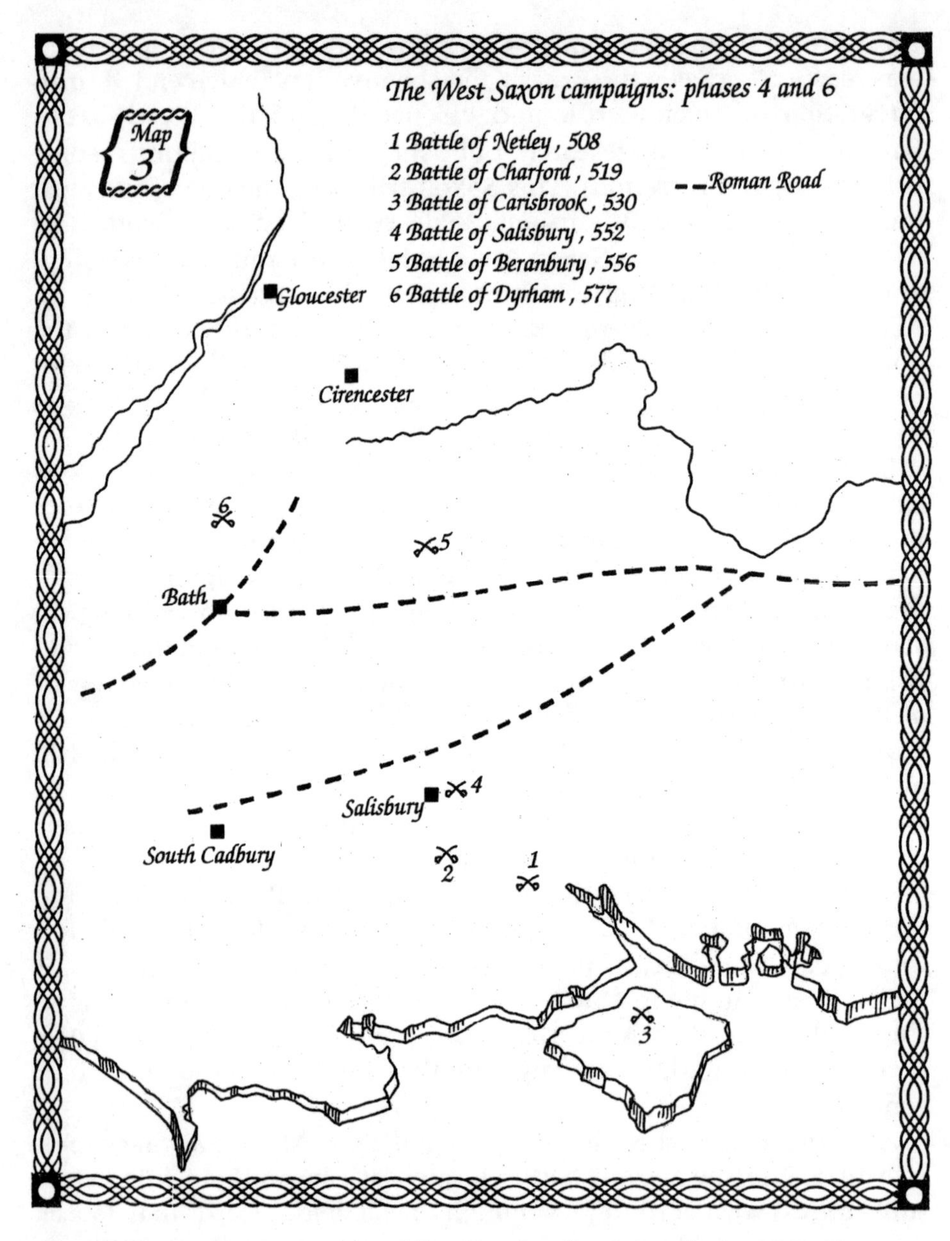


the West Saxons, occasioned by the death of Cerdic in 534. The new leader was Cynric.

At this point it must be mentioned that, in all the West Saxon activities, from the landing in 495 up to the conquest of the Isle of Wight in 530, Cerdic is specifically associated with his son Cynric. This bracketing of the two men introduces a discrepancy into the records which needs to be resolved. Earlier, when discussing the lives of the leaders of Britain in the fifth century, the concept of human life expectancy was introduced. It is needed again here. According to the *Chronicle*, Cynric was fighting alongside Cerdic at the landing in 495, at Netley in 508, at Charford in 519, at 'Cerdic's-ley' in 527 and in the Isle of Wight in 530. He fought alone at Salisbury in 552 and alongside his son Ceawlin at Barbury Castle (Barenbury in the *Chronicle*) in 556, a military career lasting 61 years in all and an overall length of life of at least 80 years. Such an extended period of life and military activity is, if not impossible, at least most unlikely.

The difficulty can be resolved if an alliterative Anglo-Saxon genealogy is used which makes Creoda the son of Cerdic, and Cynric the son of Creoda. If an active military career of 30 years is assumed for Cynric, it would then stretch back from the battle of Barbury Castle in 556 to 526. This would place his first military engagement at 'Cerdic's-ley' in 527 and his birth in the first decade of the sixth century. The reign of Cynric would extend from the death of Cerdic in 534 to the accession of Ceawlin in 560, 'twenty-six winters', as indicated in the *Chronicle*. Under this arrangement, Creoda must have died before Cerdic and some amendments must be made to the references to 'Cynric' in the *Chronicle*. The name Cynric at the landing and in the battles at Netley and Charford should be deleted or amended to read Creoda. All this could be the result of the writer of the *Chronicle* being unaware of the alliterative genealogy.

It was not until 552 that the advance of the West Saxons into Britain gained momentum. This happened when Cynric gained a decisive victory at Salisbury, ten kilometres (six miles) to the north of Charford. Four years later, in 556, and 46 kilometres (29 miles) further north at Barbury Castle, some ten kilometres (six miles) south of Swindon, Cynric and his son Ceawlin fought the British and, although victory is not claimed, it is likely that the British were defeated. This conclusion is probable because when Ceawlin succeeded his father in 560, he was, as indicated earlier, named by Bede as the second Bretwalda, in succession to Aelle, an unlikely nomination if he and his father had been defeated by the British so late in the campaign.

The most noteworthy aspect of the fourth phase is its extreme length – 61 years in total from the West Saxon landing in 495 up to the battle at Barbury Castle in 556 – and all for a penetration inland of about 67 kilometres (42 miles). This is in sharp contrast to the length of Clovis's conquest of Gaul, 21 years between the defeats of Syagrius at Soissons and that of Alaric II at Vouillé, involving a conquest stretching from the Channel to the Pyrenees.

The internal time sequence of the West Saxon campaign is also interesting in so far as it shows an acceleration in the speed of the campaign as it moves towards its end at Barbury Castle. It took 57 years and four battles for the West Saxons to move the 24 kilometres (15 miles) from the landing near Southampton to Salisbury, a long time even if allowance is made for the conquest of the Isle of Wight in 530. In took only four years and one battle to move the 46 kilometres (29 miles) from Salisbury to the victory at Barbury Castle.

As will be shown later, there is some evidence in the *Annales Cambriae* that Arthur died around the year 517. If this evidence is accepted, the slow pace of the advance from the landing in 495 to the indecisive battle at Charford in 519 could then be due to the pre-eminence of Arthur as a military leader. This superiority was established in the third phase by the 12 victories culminating in Badon and extended, as will be argued in Chapter 8, by Arthur's East Anglian campaign in the early years of the sixth century. The links between the progress of the West Saxon campaign recorded in the *Chronicle*, the quality of Arthur's leadership taken from Nennius and the report of Arthur's death in the *Annales Cambriae* (537, revised to 517), taken together, support the credibility of all three sources. In addition, this correlation, together with the linked reference to the Kentish battles in Nennius and the *Chronicle*, strengthens the belief that British and Anglo-Saxon recorders are dealing with the same events, albeit from different sides of the conflict.

The slow pace of the early West Saxon campaign is also supported by the arguments advanced earlier in favour of Castle Cadbury being the main British centre for recruitment and supply. Since Cadbury is only some 56 kilometres (35 miles) west of Charford, it is very possible that the West Saxons were held in check from 495 to 519 by the British centre of power at Cadbury, in much the same way that Aelle was held in check from 477 to 490 by Ambrosius's recruitment sites near the south coast. So great was Arthur's influence that the pace of the advance did not accelerate until the British lost heart after Salisbury in 552, more than 30 years after Arthur's death.

Ceawlin's first action after his accession to the leadership of the West Saxons in 560 was not against the British but rather to restrict the expansionist policies of Aethelbert, king of the Kentish invaders. According to Bede, Aethelbert was the great-grandson of Hengist and grandson of Aesc. He had acceded to his throne in the same year that Ceawlin had succeeded Cynric. His breakout and defeat in 568 indicated that the invaders in the Kentish bridgehead, like the South and West Saxons, had failed to move decisively against the British until the middle of the sixth century. Aethelbert's rebuff was not, however,

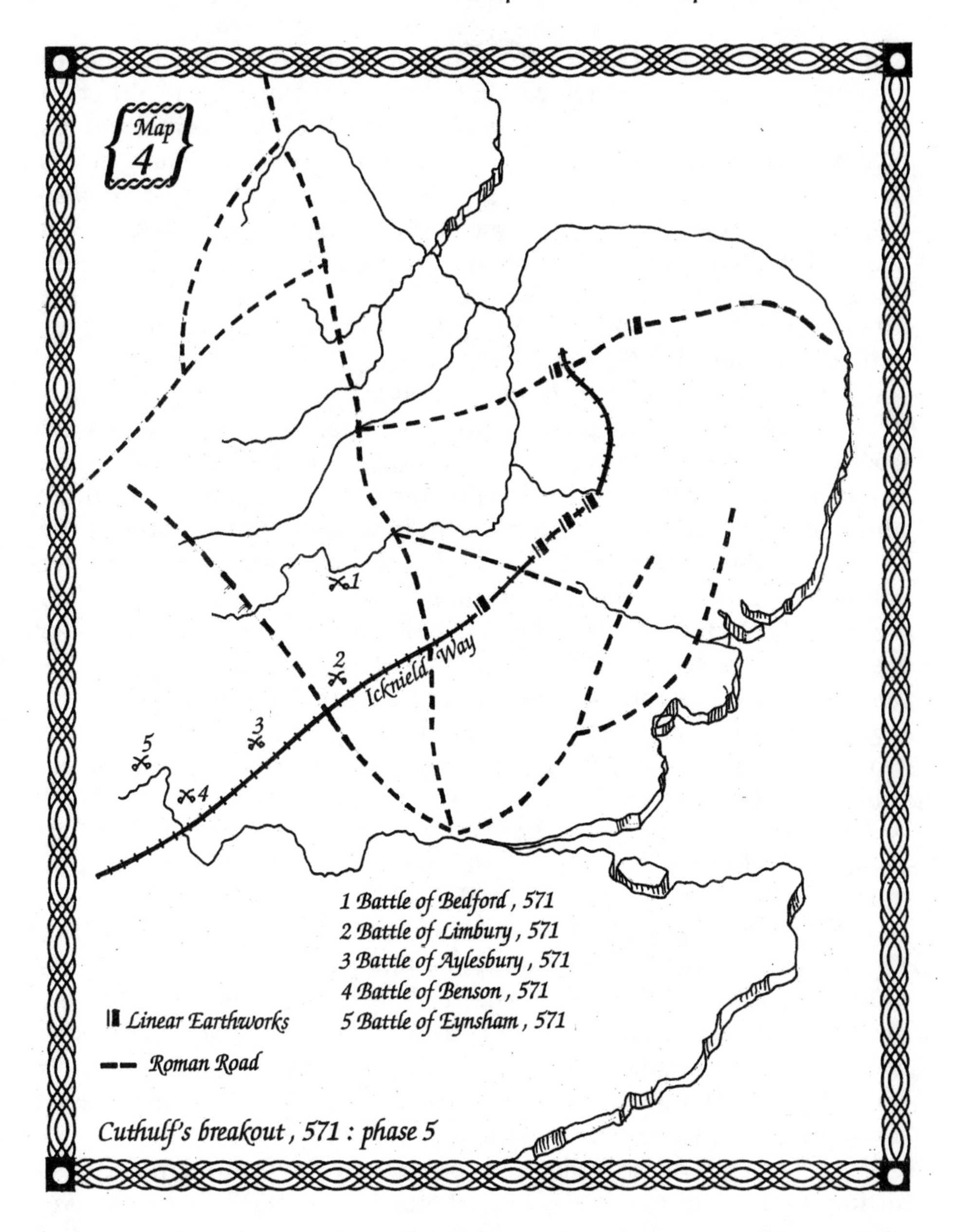

Cuthulf's breakout, 571: phase 5

to last long. He was an exceptional leader and became the next Bretwalda after the death of Ceawlin. It was he who, near the end of his long reign, was recognized by Pope Gregory as King of the English. According to the *Chronicle,* he received St Augustine in 597 and led the conversion of the invaders, the English, to Christianity.

The fact that Ceawlin managed to drive Aethelbert back into Kent demonstrated clearly that the invasion process was not always homogeneous and that rivalries existed between some of the different invading tribes. Ceawlin's victory over Aethelbert also confirmed his position as Bretwalda and gave him increased confidence in his decision to drive the remaining British even further west. It also marked the end of the fourth phase of the invasion, since at this point the West Saxons paused before any advance further westward took place. During the pause, however, another development occurred, the fifth phase, which provided Ceawlin with even more confidence in his ability to achieve his final objective.

So far, as mentioned earlier, the *Chronicle* has provided no information on the East Anglian invaders moving towards the centre of Britain from the north-east. This lack of aggression can be linked with the results of the second Arthurian campaign – the latter half of the third phase of the conquest, to be dealt with in Chapter 8. The focus of the *Chronicle* changes in 571 with a record of the achievements of a leader named Cuthulf. In this phase of the invasion process (see Map 4 on page 97) Cuthulf broke out of East Anglia and met the British, first at a place named Bedcanford, possibly Bedford, where he almost certainly defeated them, for he then advanced further south to capture the town of Limbury, near Luton. At this point he was close to the Icknield Way and, since his next objective was the town of Aylesbury, he probably advanced south-eastwards along that road to capture first Aylesbury and then Benson, not far from the place in the Goring Gap where the Icknield Way crosses the Thames. After taking Benson, he moved upstream to capture his final town from the British: Eynsham. Here he reached a point only 45 kilometres (28 miles) north-east of Barbury Castle, the site of Ceawlin's final campaign victory in his northward advance 15 years earlier in 556. Cuthulf died in the same year that his campaign started, 571, indicating a comparatively rapid advance, which must confirm the decline in British morale and their will to resist. His advance to the south-west from East Anglia embodied the penultimate part of the invasion of Britain.

The occurrence of the fifth phase so late in the invasion sequence has an important bearing on the importance of the third phase, the Arthurian campaigns. It implies that the British control of the centre of Britain did not collapse until very late in the conquest. This control, as will be argued in the next two chapters, was a direct result of Arthur's military genius.

Such a conclusion cannot easily be accepted by those historians who argue that Arthur played an insignificant part in the Anglo-Saxon conquest, and in consequence there has been a suggestion that the date of Cuthulf's victories has been misplaced in the *Chronicle* and that they should be located much earlier, perhaps even 100 years earlier, before 470. Although there is some evidence for Anglo-Saxon penetration as far as the upper Thames valley in the fifth century, their dominance in this region, implied by Cuthulf's four victories, is questionable in more than one respect.

First, the concentration of fifth-century cemeteries in the upper Thames is low compared with that in East Anglia. In the second place, the evidence of the Kentish battles between 455 and 465, provided in the *Chronicle* and supported by Nennius, suggests that Vortigern and Vortimer would not have left the Thames valley defenceless in their advance eastwards after the first major thrust to the west by the invaders. Such an advance of the British would clearly be inconsistent with Cuthulf being on the Thames before 465. A third argument against moving the four Cuthulf battles back a century is that this would be quite inconsistent with the evidence from Gildas supporting recovery under Ambrosius. It would also be inconsistent with the creation of Ambrosius's recruitment sites, which fitted well with the containment of the invaders along the south coast. Ambrosius could not, between 470 and 490, have maintained his cordon, stretching from west to east, well to the south of the Thames valley, if he had been threatened by Anglo-Saxon victories in the Oxford area at his rear. At a later date, the placing of the East Anglian victories towards the end of the fifth century or in the first half of the sixth would be incompatible with the slow progress of Cerdic in those two periods. Angles in strength on the Thames during these periods would, with the West Saxons in the south, have exerted a pincer threat to the British which would be hard to counter and difficult to correlate with Cerdic's slow progress before 552. On the other hand, the delay in the Angles' advance until 571 is not inconsistent with the argument for a second Arthurian campaign in the east, which will be developed in Chapter 8.

The accuracy of the 571 entry in the *Chronicle* is supported by all these arguments and so, consequently, is the implication that, as late as the third quarter of the sixth century, British forces remained in the centre-east of the island containing the Anglian settlements in Norfolk and Suffolk.

These British forces may well have arrived there after the battle of Badon, at the end of the third phase of the invasion sequence, and a possible reason for their location will be discussed in Chapter 8. Their destruction in 571 removed any fear that Ceawlin might have had that a thrust to the west would be hampered by a British attack at his rear.

Additionally, Cuthulf died in 571, leaving the Anglian invaders without an experienced leader, and this also would have increased the authority of Ceawlin as the Bretwalda.

The collapse of British resistance in the centre-east of the island in 571, the death of Cuthulf in the same year and the pursuit of Aethelbert back to Kent in 568 all supported Ceawlin's decision to extend his frontiers further west. After the arrival in the Thames valley of the Anglian forces from the north-east, Ceawlin made his move in the sixth and final phase of the invasion process (see Map 3 on page 94). He defeated three British kings in 577 near the small village of Dyrham, some 16 kilometres (ten miles) north of Bath, and 'took from them three cities Gloucester, Cirencester and Bath'. Following a final success in 584 at Fretherne, either in Gloucestershire or in north-east Oxfordshire, Ceawlin withdrew to the east. His reign as Bretwalda ended in disaster, for he was 'driven from his kingdom' by Ceolric in 591, in the same year as the battle at Wanborough, near Swindon. Ceawlin died in 593.

In summary, although precise dates cannot be assured, the whole six-phase invasion sequence reported in the various sources is supported by a logical pattern of interrelated events and by confidence in some key dates. The first phase is concerned with the bridgehead in Kent and with the invasion westwards led by Hengist. The British recovery was first organized by Vortigern and Vortimer, and finally by Ambrosius Aurelianus and Arthur, his successor. The end result, after about 30 years of conflict between 440 and 470, left the territorial state of Britain almost unchanged. The second phase of the campaign was led by Aelle and extended from 477 to about 490. It also had little success, for both the South Saxon invaders and Aelle's name disappear from the *Chronicle* in 490. This was almost certainly due to the start of the third phase, an entirely British resistance effort – which is dealt with in the next two chapters.

The West Saxon campaigns from 495 to 591 comprise the fourth and sixth phases of the conquest and were led by four generations of leaders: Cerdic, Creoda, Cynric and Ceawlin. The slowness of their campaigns in the first half of the sixth century coincides with the years following the British victory at Badon, firmly dated around 496. The end point of the whole conquest is fixed by Pope Gregory's recognition of Aethelbert as the King of the English. The whole invasion sequence, from the first aggression in 440 to the death of Ceawlin in 593, forms a logical progression well supported by the dates of 496 for Badon and 540 for the year in which Gildas wrote his book, living at the time somewhere in south Wales. The information in Gildas's book showed that in 540 the British were still in command of the west and probably the centre of the island, the latter being ultimately lost at a time coinciding with Gildas's death in 570, at the start of the last two phases of the conquest.

From the foregoing, it is clear that the conquest of Britain south of the Humber, excluding Wales and the far south-west, took the invading forces about 150 years, from 440 to 593. According to Gildas, these forces, or an unspecified contingent of them, 'spread from sea to sea', reaching the west coast of the island between 440 and 450. They withdrew, or were probably repelled by Vortigern and his son Vortimer. After this success, the first invaders of East Anglia and Kent and the following waves of South and West Saxons were subsequently contained in their coastal bridgeheads by Ambrosius and Arthur, and by the influence these two men exerted after their death, until the middle of the sixth century. When the breakout occurred, the rate of conquest speeded up and, by 597, was complete, apart from Wales and the south-west peninsula. Conquest on the scale of Clovis's effort had taken five times longer in Britain than in Gaul.

If the detailed structure of the campaign is examined, there is a strong likelihood that the success of the British under the leadership of Vortimer, Ambrosius and Arthur in the early phases is the probable main cause of its overall extreme length. The British campaigns led by these men occupied the middle years of the whole 150-year sequence, from about 465 to 517. In particular, the importance of the third phase is greatly enhanced, for it was then that the British recovery, started by Vortigern and Vortimer and continued by Ambrosius Aurelianus, was decisively confirmed by Arthur's victories, culminating in the battle of Badon. Consequently, although Hengist may have been superior to Vortigern in military ability in the early part of the first phase, honours were restored to even by the efforts of Vortimer and Ambrosius towards the end of this phase. Subsequently, there is little doubt that Aelle, Cerdic and Creoda were well contained by Ambrosius and Arthur in the years between 470 and 520. In the later years of the fourth phase, the West Saxon campaign, the speed of the conquest certainly accelerated coincident with Arthur's fading influence after his death around 517.

It has already been pointed out that, on the basis of age, it is extremely unlikely that the military leadership at the start of the third phase could be attributed to Ambrosius. No man could remain at the peak of his powers (needed to conduct an intensive campaign against determined invaders) from the death of Vortigern in the 460s to the end of the century. It is even more unlikely that Ambrosius could have lived into the sixth century. It is very much more probable that he handed over military control to Arthur at some time in the penultimate decade of the fifth century and that Arthur became the next High King in the last decade. As a result, in the third phase all the important successes of the British in attack, as distinct from the successes in defence achieved by Ambrosius, were almost certainly attributable to Arthur.

However, in spite of the length of the Anglo-Saxon conquest of Britain, the end result was the same as in Gaul: the invaders prevailed. Consequently, neither Arthur's military ability nor the conquest's length substantiate Arthur's importance, beyond the fact that he was chiefly responsible for a time delay, for the completion of the conquest in Britain, of about a century when compared with the duration of the Gallic conquest. It is only when the directions taken by the two new nation states of England and France are compared that important differences appear, differences which were consequential upon the interventions of the two leaders, Arthur and Clovis, and which establish the unique importance of both men.

In the case of Arthur, his importance stems from the consequences of the victories he achieved, as described in detail in the following chapters. The scale of his successes in battle was a major cause of the length of the British campaign, which disrupted the social structure of the land far more than occurred in Gaul. There the speed of the Frankish conquest left the Gallo-Roman institutions relatively undisturbed and in a position to merge with the military and social structures of the Franks. Indeed, the Gallo-Roman troops held a key position in Clovis's military organization after the defeat of Syagrius. On the other hand, in Britain, as Gildas reported, the 'cities' had been destroyed and had not been rebuilt or repopulated. During a war lasting 150 years, the successive victories and defeats, the advances and retreats, the emigration of some of the British and the troops living off the land, must all have contributed to the breakdown of social institutions and the agricultural economy. Arthur had no time to repair any of these consequences of hard-won victory before his life was ended by civil war and treachery (see Chapter 8). With no immediate British successor of any stature when compared with the military and political abilities of Ambrosius and Arthur, the Anglo-Saxons faced a land with a much-reduced military potential and an irreversibly damaged social and economic structure. These factors, and the fact that no British leader emerged who was capable of leading and coordinating the British tribes, resulted in final Anglo-Saxon victory at the end of the sixth century over what had become a political, economic and military wasteland.

There is no evidence of any integration of British and Saxon institutions, only a complete loss of national identity for those British left behind in their retreat to the west. In the land which was to become England, the residual British inhabitants, without leaders able to unite them, were quickly absorbed by their conquerors and, in the process, abandoned their language. In the event, apart from place-names, less than a dozen words of Brythonic Celtic origin can be found in the language spoken in England after the Anglo-Saxon conquest. With no military or social institutions to imitate or absorb, there was no incentive for the invaders to speak any language other than their own or to develop anything other than an Anglo-Saxon society. In the centuries which followed the conquest, the language spoken in England developed as one of the Teutonic group. Britain was the only diocese of the decaying western Roman Empire which did not develop a language falling into the Romance group based on Latin.

As Bede writes, after the mission of St Augustine, there was a progressive conversion of the largely pagan Anglo-Saxons to Christianity and, in ecclesiastical matters, a parallel reuse of Latin developed as the language of the written word. Thus there was a complete contrast in the field of linguistics between the conquests of Britain and Gaul. In Gaul, Latin as the written language existed alongside Vulgar Latin as the spoken language. The latter developed into modern French, one of the Romance group of languages. In England, the same written language, Latin, existed alongside Old English, which finally became modern English, one of the Teutonic group. In both countries, however, a written language based on the spoken language in the end completely replaced Latin, apart from vestigial traces in the law, in religious observances and in well-known phrases.

In addition to language, the development of the legal system followed a different course in Britain from that taken in Gaul, and since the law is in effect the rules of society, the difference is of major importance. In Britain, the long interregnum between the departure of the Romans and the final victory of the Anglo-Saxons in the last quarter of the sixth century ensured that any remnants of Roman Law disappeared. The military campaigns of Ambrosius and Arthur caused the decay of trade and industry and the switch to a simpler society based on agriculture which had no need of the complex system of Roman Law for its support.

After Arthur, and in the absence of a successor to the position of High King, the decay of British society continued, with no doubt a return to earlier Celtic laws, or indeed to a system with little or no law. The main theme of Gildas's book implies little justice and calls for a return to Christian values in the face of corruption of the rulers and priests in the petty British kingdoms of the West Country. The final advance of the victors to the boundaries of Wales eliminated any incentive for the invaders to adopt or adapt any Celtic laws. Consequently, the basic legal system of the Anglo-Saxons grew, little disturbed by the later Danish invasions, until the Norman conquest in 1066.

Even after this date, although English judges were well aware of the principles of Roman Law, the growing legal system remained substantially based on Anglo-Saxon foundations. Today when the phrase 'common law' is mentioned anywhere in the English-speaking world, it refers to the basic national (English or Anglo-Saxon) law as distinct from more recent laws or those derived from Roman or Continental sources. The reverse is true on the Continent of Europe, and in France in particular; there the phrase 'common law' refers to Roman Law and not the national law of the country concerned. This attitude, and all it involves in the way the law is regarded, makes another substantial difference in the direction taken by the two Roman dioceses of Britain and Gaul after the barbarian invasions.

When compared with France, the two changes in direction taken by England in the fields of language and law could perhaps be regarded as matters of detail. On a much more fundamental scale, the whole development of England after the conquest differs in nature from that in France. In England, all progress in the social, political and other fields was governed by the ideals and ideas of a Germanic group of tribes in north-western Europe with very similar, almost common, heritages. In France, on the other hand, progress was based on an amalgam of Celtic, Roman and Germanic influences and resulted in a system with much more complex antecedents, leading initially to Charlemagne's new empire of the west, which, as we have seen, excluded England. This major difference in the direction of development was the consequence, first, of the superior quality of the defence to invasion presented in Britain by Arthur and his predecessors, Ambrosius and Vortimer, and, second, to the death of Arthur before he could consolidate his success.

Summarizing, in the last two chapters it has been argued that the invasions of Gaul and Britain, two similar Roman dioceses attacked by German tribes of similar backgrounds and fighting abilities, were different in two important respects. First, although in both cases the invaders were finally successful, the length of the invasion campaigns was five times greater in Britain than in Gaul and, second, springing from this, the development of England and France after the conquests was markedly different.

With little difference in the fighting abilities of the common soldiers of the Anglo-Saxon, Frankish, Romano-British and the Gallo-Roman armies, and with a failure to find differences in the logistics faced by either of the invasion forces, the differing lengths of the two campaigns have been shown to be due to the military abilities of the opposing leaders. In the invasion of Gaul, Clovis was undeniably superior to both Syagrius and Alaric, but in Britain, as explained earlier, the British leaders, Ambrosius and Arthur, moved into the ascendant in the middle stages of the invasion sequence. A barrier to contain the invaders within their bridgeheads was created. In *The Anglo-Saxon Chronicle* the location of the early conflicts and the associated dates show that any advance inland was barred until after 520 and was very slow up to 552. The inference is clearly that, over a period of about 30 years, from 490 to 520, the influence of Arthur was pre-eminent in maintaining the Ambrosian barrier and, as will be argued in Chapter 8, in creating a new barrier in the east. It will also be claimed that his influence continued for some time after his death.

His success, coupled with his failure to eject the Anglo-Saxons, is described in detail in the next chapters. These events took the two dioceses in very different directions after the collapse of the western Roman Empire. Britain, or rather England, was in fact unique in western Europe in its preservation of a 'barbarian' culture without any Roman influence except in ecclesiastical affairs. This difference was unparalleled in the other regions of the western Roman Empire. In consequence, the importance of Arthur as a major historical figure is established, for the consequences of his action changed the very course of history.

The conclusion that a unique Anglo-Saxon development occurred in England, following Arthurian successes which could not be sustained after his death, makes it essential to find supporting evidence for the methods Arthur used. It was these methods that maintained and developed the earlier successes of Ambrosius, and led finally to an England very different from France.

# The Badon Campaign

THE ARGUMENTS presented in the previous chapter have supported both the existence and the importance of Arthur through an appeal, first, to *The Anglo-Saxon Chronicle,* Gildas, Nennius and the *Annales Cambriae* (although the two former sources do not mention Arthur by name) and, second, to a 'broad-brush' view of the differences in the historical development of England and France after the barbarian invasions. His importance was shown to arise from the fact that his effort was a prime cause for the length of the whole campaign of conquest and from the very different direction taken by the successor state of Anglo-Saxon England when compared with the direction taken by France. He achieved his importance through his military successes in phase three of the conquest. These were briefly mentioned in the previous chapter, but only in passing, as they lacked supporting evidence. They now have the support of the evidence of his importance and consequently should be examined in greater detail.

Before starting, it would be very useful to consider the transfer of power from Ambrosius to Arthur and to make some comment on the overall dating of the British events in the conquest. The sequence of the leaders of Britain during the period stretching from the accession of Vortigern in 425 to that of the Younger Ambrosius some time around 470 has been developed in Chapter 4. At the same time, the part played by Ambrosius in the second stage of the British revival was expanded from the very limited reference in Gildas to include the suggestions of Dr Morris in relation to the recruitment sites in the south of Britain. On the basis of these two historical contributions, it is very likely that the main part played by Ambrosius in the British recovery took place between 470 and 485. By the latter date the High King was probably in his mid-fifties and some 15 years into his reign.

As a sensible monarch, Ambrosius must have looked forward to the time when active military leadership would be better exercised by a younger man. The only man of whom we have any record who could fill the position of commander-in-chief is Arthur and, as indicated in Chapter 6, he was identified as the British leader in the third phase of the conquest.

Moving to the problems associated with dating, it will be appreciated that all matters relating to the ages of the British leaders have to be fitted into a sequence starting with the accession of Vortigern in 425 and ending with death of Arthur in 517. Within this period of 92 years the careers of Vortigern and his son Vortimer, the Elder and the Younger Ambrosius, and finally Arthur have to be accommodated. These five men are the only leaders named in this period and so their careers and no others must fill the whole 92 years.

Vortigern acceded in 425 and died some time after the Kentish battles of 455–65. The Elder Ambrosius was a contemporary of Vortigern and both men were very likely to have been born during the first decade of the fifth century. On a human basis, their sons Vortimer and the Younger Ambrosius were possibly born between 420 and 430. Vortimer died soon after the last Kentish battle, in 465. The Elder Ambrosius was probably 'slain' some time after Wallop and before the first Kentish battle where Vortigern was leading the British forces, between 437 and 455. Vortigern outlived his son Vortimer, for the succession passed to the Younger Ambrosius, who became the next High King, possibly around 470. Arthur, the victor at Badon in 496, died in battle in 517, suggesting a birth date around 465.

Arthur's military exploits fill the third phase of the invasion process. This phase coincides with the third stage of British recovery, following the two earlier stages, initiated by Vortigern and the Younger Ambrosius respectively. This phase is also the most important factor determining the length of the whole 150-year sequence and is uniquely associated with Arthur. Arthur's actions within this phase are those which, in the end, led to the national developments north of the Channel turning out to be very different from those to the south.

Ambrosius's successor, Arthur, took military command in the third phase and became the last overall leader of the British tribes before the Anglo-Saxon conquest changed Britain into England. All the documentary evidence will be used in the attempt to shed further light on his career, for he and his predecessor, Ambrosius, were the last heirs to the traditions established many centuries earlier by Cassivellaunus, Caratacus and Boudicca. However, because of Arthur's mixed antecedents, account has to be taken of both Celtic and Roman influences, which must have played a major role in any decisions he made.

Arthur probably took over the leadership of Britain from Ambrosius some time in the years between 480 and 490, possibly at an age of between 20 and 30. This would put his death in 517 at an age of between 50 and 60, just about young enough to take active command of his forces in his last battle. According to Nennius, it was a military type of leadership that Arthur first held, rather than a royal position. He writes: 'Then Arthur fought against them in those days, together with the kings of the British; but he was their leader in battle.' It is this reference that has cast doubt on the actual rank held by Arthur – in particular whether or not he was 'King Arthur'. However, he could have become the 'leader of battles' or commander-in-chief before Ambrosius's death and only succeeded as High King after the Younger Ambrosius died. This sequence would fit well with a naturally ageing Ambrosius and with the even higher rank of 'emperor' given to Arthur in the later poem 'Elegy of Geraint', mentioned in Chapter 1. Arthur could indeed have become High King (or even emperor, in the eyes of his enthusiastic followers, harking back to the days of imperial Roman rule and to the precedents set by Constantine III, Magnus Maximus and Carausius), at some time during the great campaign described in Nennius which ended with the battle of Badon in 496. By this time the probability of Ambrosius's death would be almost a certainty.

Although Arthur's mentor was the Younger Ambrosius and although he, like both the Elder and the Younger Ambrosius, probably wished to see a return to at least some of the Roman traditions, account had to be taken of the regrowth of Celtic concepts which had occurred during Vortigern's reign. Consequently, when Arthur became the supreme military leader of the Romano-British forces, he would almost certainly have been following the pattern set by earlier Celtic leaders in Britain and by Vercingetorix in Gaul. He would have had to persuade the tribal kings and leaders to unite under his command in the face of a dangerous enemy. He would not, therefore, have possessed the supreme authority held by a Roman *imperator* when Rome was in danger.

There are only two documents which give any indication of his achievements. The first is the *Annales Cambriae,* in which there are just two relevant entries. Under the date 516 the text reads: 'The battle of Badon, in which Arthur carried the Cross of our Lord Jesus Christ for three days and three nights on his shoulders and the British were the victors.' (The word 'shoulders' is probably a mistranslation of the original text and should read 'shield'. In early Welsh, *scuid* – shoulder – is similar to *scuit* – shield.)

Under the date 537 the second entry reads: 'The battle of Camlann, in which Arthur and Medraut fell; and there was a plague in Britain and Ireland.'

The date in the *Annales Cambriae* for Badon is 20 years later than the date given in Chapter 4, which was provided by Gildas in one of his more precise statements. Since the 496 date is now generally preferred, it would be acceptable to move the Camlann date by the same amount and place the battle and the death of Arthur in 517, the date given in earlier chapters.

There is general agreement that the *Annales* are a reliable source and consequently they provide one new personal name, Medraut, and the name of one new battle, Camlann. Both will be dealt with in the next chapter. The first entry, however, provides confirmation of Gildas's reference to the important battle of Badon, which is also described in the second document.

This second document has already been mentioned in Chapter 6. It is Chapter 56 of Nennius's book and provides details of all the campaign battles leading up to Badon. The relevant paragraph appears immediately following the sentence in which Arthur is described as the leader in battle. These 12 engagements form the first part of the third phase of the invasion sequence and Nennius claims that Arthur was victorious in all of them.

There is substantial agreement that the list is a prose rendering of a bardic poem and its importance results from two factors. First, the final battle is that at Badon, for which there is independent confirmation in both the *Annales Cambriae* and Gildas. Second, the battle of Camlann is omitted and it has been argued that, because of the melancholy nature of early Welsh poetry, it is almost impossible for Camlann not to have been mentioned if it had taken place when the poem was declaimed. As a result of this, it can be concluded that the poem was composed soon after Badon had been fought and is thus most likely to have been recited in Arthur's lifetime in his honour and, very possibly, in his presence. It is therefore likely to be both contemporary and accurate. For this reason the text is quoted in full:

> The first battle was at the mouth of the river called Glein. The second, the third, the fourth and the fifth were on another river, called the Dubglas, which is in the region Linnuis. The sixth battle was on the river called Bassas. The seventh battle was in the forest of Celidon, that is the battle of Celidon Wood. The eighth battle was in Guinnion Fort, and in it Arthur carried the image of the holy Mary, the everlasting Virgin, on his shoulder [once again, probably 'shield'], and the heathen were put to flight on that day, and there was a great slaughter among them through the power of Our Lord Jesus Christ and the power of the

> holy Virgin Mary, his mother. The ninth battle was fought in the city of the Legion. The tenth battle was fought on the bank of the river called Tribruit. The eleventh battle was on the hill called Agned. The twelfth battle was on Badon Hill and in it nine hundred and sixty men fell in one day, from a single charge of Arthur and no one laid them low save he alone; and he was victorious in all his battles.

These 12 battles are the constituent parts of Arthur's first great campaign and form perhaps the most critical component of the invasion sequence. The victories claimed strongly support the concept of Arthur's military competence, always provided the record is accepted as historically trustworthy. Unfortunately, not much detail is provided apart from the useful information that seven of the battles were fought on or near rivers, two on hills, two near forts and one in a forest. For two of the engagements, at Guinnion Fort and at Badon Hill, there is a little additional data. In both battles Arthur carried Christian emblems on his shield and in both the casualties among his opponents were exceptionally high.

Before dealing with the campaign in detail, battle by battle, it is worth considering the possible composition of the forces at Arthur's disposal, and these must have depended to a large extent on Arthur's view of the military requirements of the campaign. His decisions on the type of military force must have been conditioned by his experience. It is almost certain that, before becoming commander-in-chief, he served under the Younger Ambrosius and would thereby have learned of the difficulties of governing a country and leading its military forces, where Roman and Celtic influences existed side by side – and perhaps clashed.

Ambrosius, following his father, was a supporter of the Roman view of society, but many of the local kings, following Vortigern's lead, had, over the years of the fifth century, moved away from Rome towards a more Celtic way of life. Both Ambrosius, the High King, and Arthur, his military commander-in-chief in the late fifth century, needed to hold the country together and consequently had to reconcile the two aspects of the society in which they lived, the Roman and the Celtic. Although, as indicated earlier, the absolute authority of a Roman general was impossible to achieve in those days, Ambrosius and Arthur, being sensible men, would no doubt have tried to take advantage of the best features of both Roman and Celtic expertise in military matters.

One of the most important Roman concepts, which Arthur would certainly have appreciated, was a late trend in Roman military command organization in Britain which was recorded just before the officials were expelled in the early years of the fifth century. As explained in Chapter 3, the *Notitia Dignitatum* described three separate commands used in the defence of the province of Britannia. These three were the Duke of the Britains, the Count of the Saxon Shore and the Count of the Britains. This organization would certainly have been known to the Elder Ambrosius and passed on to his son and so to Arthur.

Both Ambrosius and Arthur would have realized that there was no possibility of providing a static garrison force in the north. The ground structures of forts and camps had fallen into disrepair and the infrastructure needed by such forces, such as sources of military rations or equipment, were unavailable. There was consequently no real place for a Duke of the Britains. With one exception, to be considered in the next chapter, the coastal forts in the east and south had been taken or bypassed by the Anglo-Saxons and thus the post of Count of the Saxon Shore was also superfluous. The third command, Count of the Britains, was, however, a concept very relevant to late fifth-century Britain.

This third command reflected the changed Roman attitude to cavalry, which was crystallized by the disaster at Adrianople in 378, the first occasion when the Roman infantry was decisively beaten by cavalry. In the forces allocated to the Count of the Britains, there were more cavalry regiments than infantry, to provide that mobility of response not available to either the Duke of the Britains or the Count of the Saxon Shore. With all of Britain south of Hadrian's Wall to defend and with Anglo-Saxon attacks likely to come from any part of a long coastline, the possession of a mobile cavalry force must have been very attractive to Arthur.

Ambrosius placed emphasis on a ring of recruitment sites in southern Britain to contain expansion inland from the coastal bridgeheads, but all of these could hardly have been effectively garrisoned on a permanent basis; the weakened state of the country would not have supported them. At best they would have served as early warning stations to sound the alarm if any penetration inland was attempted by the invaders. In any case, they were located at fixed sites and were therefore ill suited to meet ever-increasing attacks from unexpected quarters. The limitation in the value of the recruitment sites must have added to the incentive for Arthur to recruit a mobile cavalry force which could respond rapidly where danger threatened.

In addition, the excitement and intoxication of a cavalry charge would have appealed to the Celtic instincts of a warrior, much as the chariot and cavalry charges had appealed to the Celtic troops of

Cassivellaunus some 400 years earlier. Both Roman experience and Celtic feeling would have persuaded Arthur to organize his forces on the lines of the cavalry units of the Count of the Britains. Lines from 'Elegy for Geraint', the Welsh poem mentioned earlier which described a battle in the last two decades of the fifth century, support the view that cavalry undertook a major role in the British forces. It is possible that this battle poem can be linked with the *Chronicle* reference to an attack on Portsmouth in the year 501:

> Under the thigh of Geraint swift chargers,
> Long their legs, wheat their fodder,
> Red, swooping like milk white eagles.

In addition, the distribution of battle sites in the Nennius extract, seven on rivers and two on hills out of a total of 12, suggests that Arthur's cavalry played a decisive role; forcing an enemy back against a river bank or subjecting him to the terror of a downhill cavalry charge are two particularly effective cavalry tactics.

In contrast to the British forces, it is unlikely that the Anglo-Saxons used cavalry. The transport of horses across the North Sea would have been impracticable on any useful scale and indeed the presence of horse gear in the invaders' graves is rare. The tactical advantage of Arthur's cavalry over the Anglo-Saxon infantry would have been most felt in dealing with incursions of war bands of infantry moving out of the bridgeheads into central Britain. However, as will be explained later, this advantage would have been reversed into a disadvantage if the cavalry was sent to attack fortified sites within the bridgeheads.

In Chapter 6 it was claimed that there was no evidence of substantial difference in military gear or techniques between the contending forces. At this later stage of the conflict, there is both direct and circumstantial evidence that the genius of one leader, Arthur, reintroduced light cavalry to the Romano-British forces which gave a decisive advantage under some circumstances.

The situation in Britain at the end of the fifth century would also have had some bearing on the size of the forces involved. There would have been no place for military units of the size of the Roman legion in the province in the fifth century. Such units could no longer be sustained in Britain. Following the fragmentation of the country under petty kings during this century, it would have been most unlikely that any of them could muster more than a few hundred warriors. It is therefore also unlikely that the force with which, as Nennius reports, 'Arthur fought against them, together with the kings of the British, but he was their leader in battle', was much larger than 1,000 or 2,000 men.

The efficiency of military units depends on equipment as well as on size. After the departure of Roman troops from Britain at the turn of the century in support of the Continental ambitions of Constantine III, and after the ejection of the remaining Roman officials, there were probably very few, if any, Roman units left in the land. In parallel with this decline, the military specialist services also disappeared; the armourers, engineers and other craftsmen, no longer needed in Britain, moved to the Continent. As a consequence, steel armour and chain mail gradually disappeared, to be replaced by thick leather protection. The number of swords also declined and the number of lances increased. For these reasons, apart from the differences resulting from the use of cavalry by the British, there was substantial parity between the military equipment of invaders and defenders.

There is therefore much information which leads to a fairly accurate estimate of the composition and nature of the forces led both by Arthur and by the leaders of the Anglo-Saxons. The historical documents, however, give no specific details of the battle plans on either side. A first step towards discovering the nature of these plans would be to attempt to identify the sites of the battles mentioned in the campaign sequence in terms of modern geography. Because the Nennius text and the entries in the *Annales Cambriae* are the only historical documents specifically mentioning Arthur's battles, the sites listed there must form the basis of any attempted identification of a consistent campaign plan. One of the most comprehensive attempts to locate the sites is that provided by Professor Alcock (1971: 61) and his very detailed analysis is summarized in the following paragraph.

The sixth, eighth and tenth battles, on the River Bassas, at Guinnion Fort and on the River Tribruit respectively, were not identified with any modern site but some possible localities were found for the remaining nine battles. The first battle, on the River Glein, sets a pattern for all nine in that there is more than one possible location for the engagement. The word Glein or Glen, as applied to rivers, can be derived from a British word meaning 'pure' or 'clean', and there are two rivers with the name Glen, one in south Lincolnshire and one in Northumberland. There may have been more in those early times. The second, third, fourth and fifth battles are on a river called Dubglas in the region Linnuis. The word Dubglas, meaning 'blue-black', is very little help to the problem of location, but the name Linnuis is more useful. Taking into account possible errors in manuscript lettering, there are three possible regions: one is in Lincolnshire (Lincoln was known as Lindum in Roman times); a second Linnuis was mentioned by the geographer Ptolemy and located north of the Clyde; and the third is in the area around Ilchester in the south-west. The seventh battle in the Forest of Celidon certainly took place in Scotland and could be placed just north of Carlisle or north of the Clyde–Forth line, with a slight margin in favour of the former. The ninth battle, in the City of the Legion, could be located either at Chester-on-Dee or at Caerleon-on-Usk, both of which were legionary fortresses. The eleventh battle on a hill called Agned (or Breguoin in some manuscripts) could be located at places as far apart as the Roman fort of Bremenium, just below the Cheviot Hills, or at Bravonium, a British-Latin place-name, which has been identified with Leintwardine in Herefordshire. Finally, there are several suggested sites for the last and most important battle on Badon Hill. One group of possible sites comes from the identification of Badon as a form of Badbury or 'Badda's fort' and there are five Badburys in a line stretching from Dorset to Lincolnshire. As an alternative, another possible site comes from the Welsh tradition which identifies Badon with Bath and perhaps places the battle on one of the hills overlooking that city.

As a result of Alcock's analysis the possible sites for the battles in Arthur's campaign are spread across the length and breadth of the island, from Scotland in the north to Somerset in the south and from Caerleon in the west to Lincolnshire in the east. Because the battle sites are so widely spread across Britain, and because there is more than one possible site for most of them, a coherent plan for the campaign is still not apparent, although such a plan would be most valuable in view of the importance of the campaign.

Before moving forward in the attempt to formulate such a plan, an important point should be made. As explained in Chapter 6, *The Anglo-Saxon Chronicle* places many of the battles it records in the late fifth and early sixth centuries in a date order which also corresponds with a clear geographical sequence. For example, the battles of Netley Marsh, Charford, Salisbury and Barbury Castle are in date order and in the appropriate location sequence for a military campaign moving progressively from Southampton Water northwards to Barbury Castle, near Swindon. There is no reason to doubt that the British were as capable as the Anglo-Saxons in reporting battles in the correct order in both space and time. In any case, even if dates were inappropriate to a battle poem, the unknown bard would hardly dare to place the battles in any other than the proper geographical and time sequence when he was declaiming the poem before the victorious king himself. Gildas declares Badon to be the final victory and here at least there is proof that the bard correctly placed the right battle at the end of the sequence. It will therefore be assumed in the later discussion that the battles in the Nennius text are in the correct time sequence and in positions which are acceptable from a military and geographic point of view.

The success of the whole campaign, especially at Badon, the final battle, and the indication in *The Anglo-Saxon Chronicle* of the clear inability of the invaders to make much progress inland until the middle of the sixth century, both demonstrate the superior qualities of Arthur as a military leader. This being so, it is inconceivable that he would not have had an overall campaign plan, naturally based on past achievements and future intentions. The plan would also conform to a strategy dictated by military efficiency.

At the outset the campaign could be planned with little restriction on Arthur's movements. He could, for example, move north in the knowledge that his rear would be protected by Ambrosius, a High King with considerable military experience. In any case, it is unlikely that an experienced military leader such as Ambrosius would contemplate a campaign going as far north as Scotland if he was not certain that the invaders in the south of England could be held at bay. Consequently, Arthur's campaign would never have been initiated unless Ambrosius was confident of his own ability to hold the line in the south.

Arthur could also have built on the success gained by Ambrosius, who had, through his recruitment policies, made it possible to restrain the invaders within the confines of the coastal areas. He would also have supported Ambrosius's commitment to the plan of the Elder Ambrosius for the restoration of some sort of Roman authority to the whole of Roman Britain. He would have realized that this could now be achieved only by expelling the Anglo-Saxon invaders from the east and south, and the Irish from the west, for much of Wales had been colonized by the Irish in the fifth century. These objectives would certainly have appealed to a young military leader such as Arthur.

His belief in his own ability to meet these objectives would also have been sustained by information reaching him from across the Channel. Britain was still not completely isolated from the Continent, for even after the imperial link was broken, in the early years of the fifth century, traders and travellers crossed the Channel and brought over Continental news. Both Ambrosius and Arthur might have been discouraged by the defeat of Syagrius by Clovis, but would have been encouraged by the knowledge that Syagrius's father, Aegidius, an experienced military commander, had carved out a semi-Roman state in northern Gaul and held it during his lifetime.

Arthur's campaign ended in 496, the best date for Badon, and, taking into account the wide range of battle locations, the whole campaign could well have spread over a period of several years. A possible date for the start of the campaign would then lie around the year 490, which fits reasonably with the end of Ambrosius's military career between 485 and 490. At the start of his campaign, the first in all probability where he exercised sole command, Arthur would have very likely been aged between 20 and 30.

The errors in these dates and ages could perhaps be plus or minus a few years in each case, but the need to reconcile them with each other, with the firm dates in the historical records and with the life expectancy of British leaders argued earlier in this chapter makes the values put forward very feasible.

The suggestion that Ambrosius was still alive at the start of Arthur's campaign, since his presence was needed to retain some control of the south while Arthur moved north, supports Arthur's commission as *dux bellorum*, the leader of battles, rather than king. However, the success at Badon probably occurred after Ambrosius's death and so left the way open for Arthur to become the next High King, before the last battle of the campaign. He would, however, still be described by the bard as 'leader of battles', even if the poem was declaimed before his royal court, for that is just what he was throughout the longer part of his great campaign.

Consequently, some time between the years 485 and 490, Arthur must have planned and initiated his campaign to recover the whole island of Britain from the Anglo-Saxons and the Irish, the former being the chief enemy. He must have had some knowledge of the situation he faced. In the first place, he knew the South Saxons were present in some force on the south coast and were led by Aelle – although here the invaders had made little progress inland. In Kent Hengist's son Aesc was consolidating his position, either during the last years of his father's life or just after his father's death in 488. Aesc also needed a period of recovery after the turbulence caused by Vortimer's campaign about 20 years earlier.

In addition, Arthur must have known that the Angles in Norfolk and Suffolk were still there in force and had been allowed to consolidate their position since the early years of the fifth century. There were also Anglo-Saxon incursions into Lincolnshire and possibly further north, and there was still some danger from beyond Hadrian's Wall and from Irish raiders on the west coast.

The earlier argument that Arthur would have opted for a cavalry force resembling that of the Count of the Britains is now reinforced by the recognizable presence of so many danger points near and far. The predominant need for high mobility, linked with the lack of technical services from competent armourers, would, however, have led to light cavalry being used, rather than the heavy cavalry with the protective armour found in the eastern Roman army.

For such a campaign against so many enemies, Arthur would have needed, in addition to mobile cavalry, a well-protected base out of range of Saxon raids for the purpose of recruiting, resting and training his forces. This base would have been in the south or south-west of Britain and would also have been Ambrosius's headquarters – two such bases would be most unlikely. As described in Chapter 1, the fort at South Cadbury would be an ideal site for such a base, which, if used by Ambrosius, could have been reconstructed and improved by Arthur after he had become High King at some time between 490 and 500.

As an intelligent and able military commander, Arthur would have carefully constructed his tactical, as distinct from strategic, plan to get maximum results from minimum effort. The war effort, which had already lasted from the year 440 almost to the end of the century, must have seriously depleted the resources of the country. For this reason, he would obviously have used the Roman roads (which would still have been in reasonable condition) as far as he could to get supplies and replacements from his base as quickly as possible. Use of the roads would also have provided a powerful aid to mobility. He could then have selected his geographic objectives and placed them in a logical order to avoid unnecessary meandering across the country.

It is not possible to know with any certainty what his strategic plan was, but an approach can be made to the problem. It is possible to decide what a competent military commander might plan to do and then compare the result with the information available on the campaign sequence.

Arthur had to face three enemies and to attempt their destruction. The first and main enemies were the invading tribes from the Continent: the Saxons along the south and east coasts, the Jutes in Kent and the Angles in Norfolk, Suffolk, Lincolnshire and north of the Humber. The second, and probably the least important, due to Hengist's efforts, were to be found north of Hadrian's Wall: the Scots, who had invaded from Ireland, and the Picts. Finally, the west coast of Britain, from the north to the south of Wales, had been invaded by Irish tribes.

Three strategic military objectives spring to mind which could be used by any military commander faced with a situation such as that facing Arthur: first, to divide the enemy and so defeat them piecemeal;

second, to invest and destroy as many enemy centres as possible in order to persuade them to leave the country; and, finally, to show the flag. This last objective would be used in an attempt to convince the invaders that the British were able and willing to assert their control over all Britain south of Hadrian's Wall. These three objectives, together with the location of the three enemy areas and the layout of the Roman roads, will, in what follows, be used to construct a coherent overall battle sequence which will be seen to match well with the specific information in the Nennius record, and also with the problems facing Arthur at the start of his campaign in or around 490.

Like that of any competent military general, Arthur's prime target would certainly have been to attack his main enemies, the invaders from the Continent, first. He had a choice, however, in deciding in which area to initiate the 'divide and conquer' plan. He could divide Aesc and the Jutes in Kent from Aelle and the South Saxons on the south coast, or, as a second option, Aesc from the Angles and Saxons in Norfolk, Suffolk and Essex. He had a third option of dividing the Angles by directing his first thrust between their two main areas in East Anglia and Lincolnshire.

On the evidence of *The Anglo-Saxon Chronicle*, the South Saxons had made little progress at this time. Although Aelle had landed in 477, he was still fighting on the coast near Pevensey in 490. Consequently, there would have been no pressing need to divide the Kentish tribes from such a minor incursion at this stage, and, in any case, the headquarters troops left behind in South Cadbury under Ambrosius's command could have been relied upon to limit any activity on the south coast. The Kentish tribes were also firmly separated from the Angles and Saxons to the north by the Thames estuary and by Ambrosius's recruitment sites in Essex. In addition, Aesc had recently succeeded Hengist as king in Kent (in 488) and was no doubt looking forward to consolidating his position, rather than renewing the attack on the British. As a result, direct action on Arthur's part in this area would also have been given lower priority.

It was a different situation to the north, in the region of the Wash. Here evidence from the cemeteries indicates heavy concentrations of invaders in the early fifth century in both Lincolnshire and East Anglia. A link between these two areas could have led to a potential power base for an attack on central Britain from the north-east. The hoped-for Roman restoration might then have been subjected to a pincer attack from the Angles in the north-east and from Aelle and Aesc in the south and south-east.

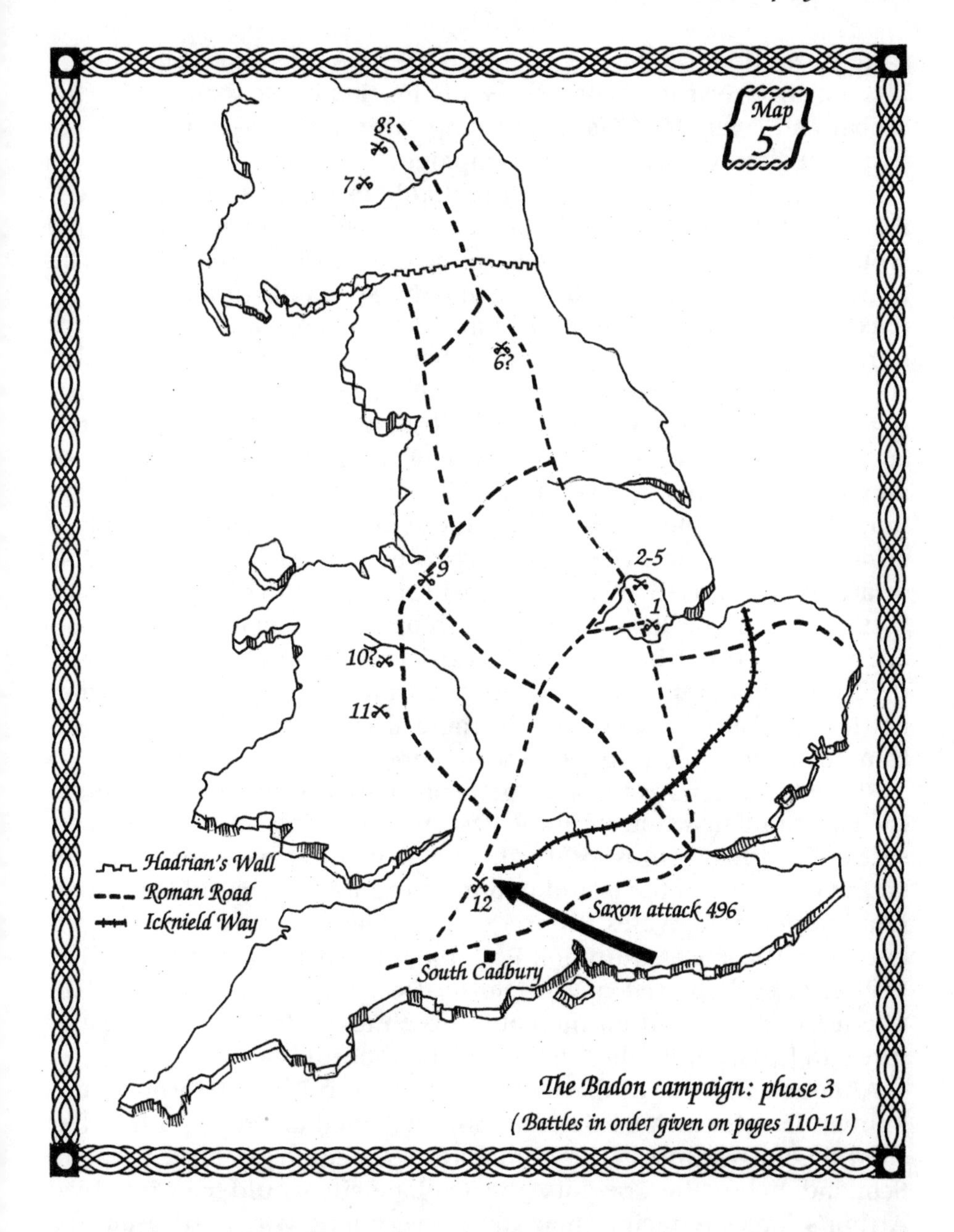


*The Badon campaign: phase 3*
*(Battles in order given on pages 110-11)*

Faced with this situation, it is very likely that Arthur's first point of attack in the campaign would have been between Lincolnshire and East Anglia. This choice is supported by his knowledge that the Fosse Way, a major Roman road, passed a few kilometres north of the base at South Cadbury and led directly to Lincoln. It is also in accord with the site of the first battle of the campaign on the Lincolnshire river Glen (see Map 5 on page 119). It is thus probable that the Lincolnshire river is a more likely site for this battle than the Northumberland river. There is strong support on military grounds for its being the first battle site of the campaign.

After the decision on the most probable location of the first battle, the sites of the next, the group of four battles in the district of Linnuis, would naturally be those closest to the Lincolnshire River Glen. The Linnuis sites in the south-west and in Scotland, then, would be rejected in favour of the one in Lincolnshire, only a few kilometres north of the first battle. There are other reasons supporting the Lincolnshire choice. The Ilchester site would have involved Arthur retracing his steps all the way down the Fosse Way to the West Country, and, in any case, there is no evidence of Anglo-Saxon penetration so far west at this time. Nor is it likely that four battles would have been fought north of the Forth–Clyde line when the Scots posed only a minor threat to the Britain of Ambrosius and Arthur south of Hadrian's Wall. Additionally, leaving aside the unknown site of the sixth battle on the River Bassas, the seventh battle in the Forest of Celidon can be located north of Carlisle, and would have been all that was necessary to subdue the minor threat from the north. The Celidon battle would also have been on the route of a natural progression north from the River Glen through Lincolnshire.

Since Arthur, in his first engagements, had directed his attention to the Germanic invasion from the east by advancing north on the east side of Britain, it is most probable that he would have returned south on the west side of the island in order to address the problem of Irish immigration into Wales. Consequently, again passing over the unknown battle site at Guinnion Fort, the ninth battle at the City of the Legion is well placed at Chester-on-Dee, nearer to Scotland than Caerleon-on-Usk and on the natural path towards the second major threat to Britain from the Irish invaders in north Wales.

Although the site of the tenth battle on the River Tribruit is unknown, the eleventh battle at the hill of Agned or Breguoin is better sited at Leintwardine in Herefordshire, to the south of Chester, than in Scotland, below the Cheviots (the Scotland site would have involved Arthur's forces retracing their steps a very long way north from the City of the Legion). Finally, if the site of the twelfth battle was chosen near Bath, it would be almost in a direct line between Leintwardine and base headquarters at South Cadbury.

These arguments, based on the location of Arthur's three potential enemies and on the efficiency of movement of Arthur's forces, allow a choice of the most probable route which Arthur followed in the course of his great campaign (see Map 5 on page 119). The result is a sequence of engagements in accord with the Nennius list of battles, where the overall plan is efficient in avoiding needless retracing of steps and is also in agreement with a clear strategic plan underlying the whole campaign.

A further result is that the three sites which cannot be located on philological grounds, the battles on the River Bassas, at Guinnion Fort and on the River Tribruit, may now be approximately located between the sites of the battles which precede and follow them. The River Bassas could thus be one of the rivers in Yorkshire, Durham or Northumberland. Guinnion Fort could be one of the Roman forts between Celidon Wood and Chester. The fact that the enemy at Guinnion Fort was pagan suggests that the location could be on the eastern side of Britain, in a fort captured by the Anglo-Saxons. The north-west of Britain had, by the end of the fifth century, become the British kingdom of Rheged, ruled by a descendant of Coel, of 'Old King Cole' fame, and was more likely to be an ally than an enemy of Arthur. Finally, the battle at the River Tribruit can be placed between Chester and Leintwardine, very possibly where the Roman road from Chester through Leintwardine to Caerleon crosses the Severn near Wroxeter.

It is interesting to note that an earlier attempt to locate the Arthurian battle sites was made over 100 years ago by W. F. Skene. He made a case for placing Arthur and his campaigns in Scotland and, to this end, found sites for all 12 battles north of the border. Some of these locations (see Map 6 on page 122) coincide with those in Alcock's comprehensive list, but most do not.

For the first battle Skene finds another River Glein in Ayrshire and prefers it to the Northumberland river in England. For the next four battles, following Ptolemy, he prefers the Linnuis site in Scotland, which he identifies with the district of Lennox. He sites the four battles on the River Dubglas all on the hill Ben Arthur, which lies between the two rivers, the Upper and Lower Douglas (Dubglas), as they fall into Loch Lomond. Since there is no River Bassas in either Scotland or England in modern times, Skene uses the derivation of the word *bass*, a small hill naturally formed near a river, to place the sixth battle on the River Dunipace, where there are two such hills. The last syllable of 'Dunipace' he identifies with *bass*. As with Alcock, the seventh battle in Celidon Wood is placed north of Carlisle and, more precisely, on the Upper Tweed. The suggestion that a fragment of the cross of the crucifixion is preserved in Wedale, and the derivation of Wedale as the 'dale of woe' where a Saxon disaster is remembered, coupled with Nennius's report that Arthur carried a religious emblem

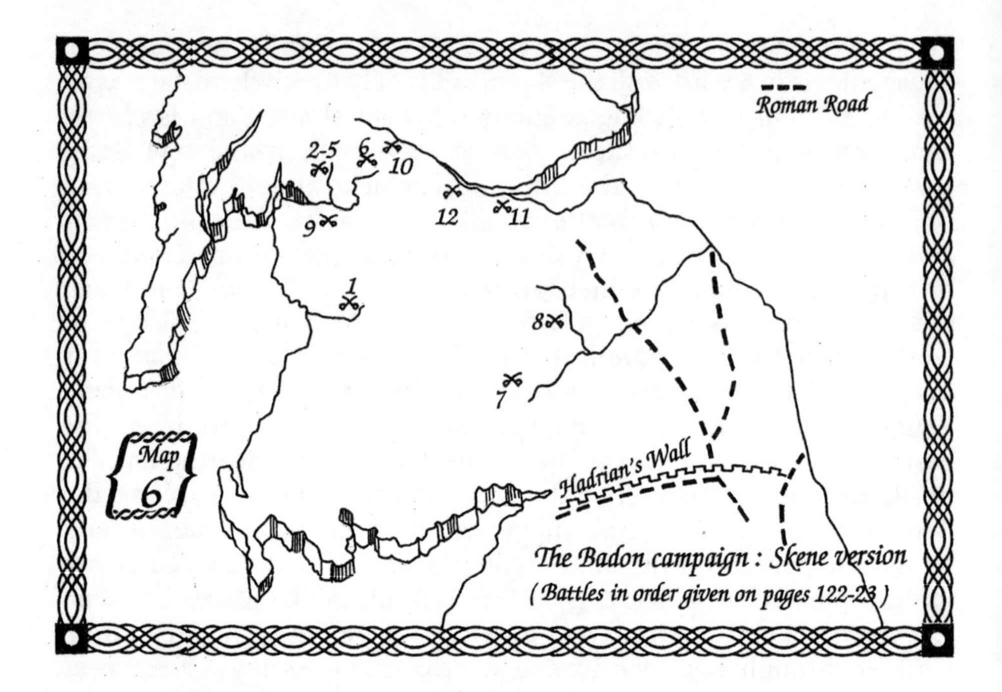


in the eighth battle, all enable Skene to place this engagement near Stow-in-Wedale. There is a Roman fort nearby, which could be Nennius's Guinnion Fort, an additional point in favour of Skene's location of this battle. His sites for the seventh and eighth battles are the only two of his proposals which are compatible with the plan for the complete battle sequence proposed in Map 5 (see page 119).

Skene's siting of the next two battles is not so sure. While admitting the possibility of the ninth battle being placed at either Caerleon or Chester, Skene prefers to use Nennius's list of the 'Wonders of Britain' and places the battle at Dumbarton. A very complex philological argument is used to place the tenth battle at Stirling. Finally, the eleventh battle on the hill Agned is identified as Mynyd Agned, or Edinburgh, and the twelfth battle is placed on Bouden Hill, not far from Linlithgow.

Unlike Alcock, who supplies alternative locations for most of the battles, Skene names only one site for each battle. This leads to a fixed route which Arthur must have followed in Scotland. As a consequence, this route has to be associated with the strategic plan which Arthur must have used in his campaign. Examination of the route in Map 6 (see page 122), using the same assumption that the battles are in the correct order, makes it difficult to devise any plan which a man of Arthur's competence might have used. It is most uneconomic in military effort, crossing and recrossing as it does from east to west of Scotland within a very narrow 64-kilometre (40-mile) band from Loch Lomond in the north to Kilmarnock in the south. The closeness of the battle sites probably means that Arthur was engaging and defeating relatively small bands of the enemy. The implication is that Arthur's most memorable campaign was entirely devoted to an enemy in a small area of Scotland some 480 or 640 kilometres (300 or 400 miles) to the north of much more dangerous enemies. The Anglo-Saxons were holding bridgeheads in East Anglia and Kent and were energetically attacking the south coast of England. The Irish were busy invading Wales. Such neglect of obvious military dangers must cast doubt on Arthur's competence as a military leader, but these doubts are completely at variance with Arthur's bardic reputation and with his importance as the major factor responsible for extending the length of the main Anglo-Saxon conquest sequence, which was located south of the Humber. For all these reasons, the campaign route in Map 5 (see page 119) is far more likely to represent Arthur's strategic plan than the route in Map 6 (see page 122).

The allocation of probable sites for the battles suggested here (as distinct from the Scottish list) makes it possible to examine each battle in turn in order to discover reasons for its location, the part it played in the overall campaign and how it fitted the simple strategic plans that have been assumed.

Initially, as Arthur left South Cadbury and proceeded north-east up the Fosse Way, he would have had little to fear from attack on his right flank. There he was protected by the natural barrier of the Thames valley and by the threat which Ambrosius imposed to the invaders in the south. As indicated above, Aelle and Aesc were in no position to attack. Just north of Leicester, Arthur could have left the Fosse Way by another Roman road leading eastward to Threekingham, on the main Roman road from London to Lincoln. At that point, a decision would have had to be made: whether to move north, towards a large concentration of the invaders in Lincolnshire, or south, towards the East Anglian settlements. For a capable general there could be no doubt of the preferred direction: to move north at this stage would have left a powerful and aggressive enemy force in his rear. He would consequently have taken the Threekingham road preparatory to a move against the invaders in Norfolk (see Map 7 on page 124).

Some 24 kilometres (15 miles) south of Threekingham the Lincoln–London road leads into the bow of the River Glen just south of Bourne, where the river, which flows south-east from its source, changes direction and flows north-east into the River Welland. It is likely that

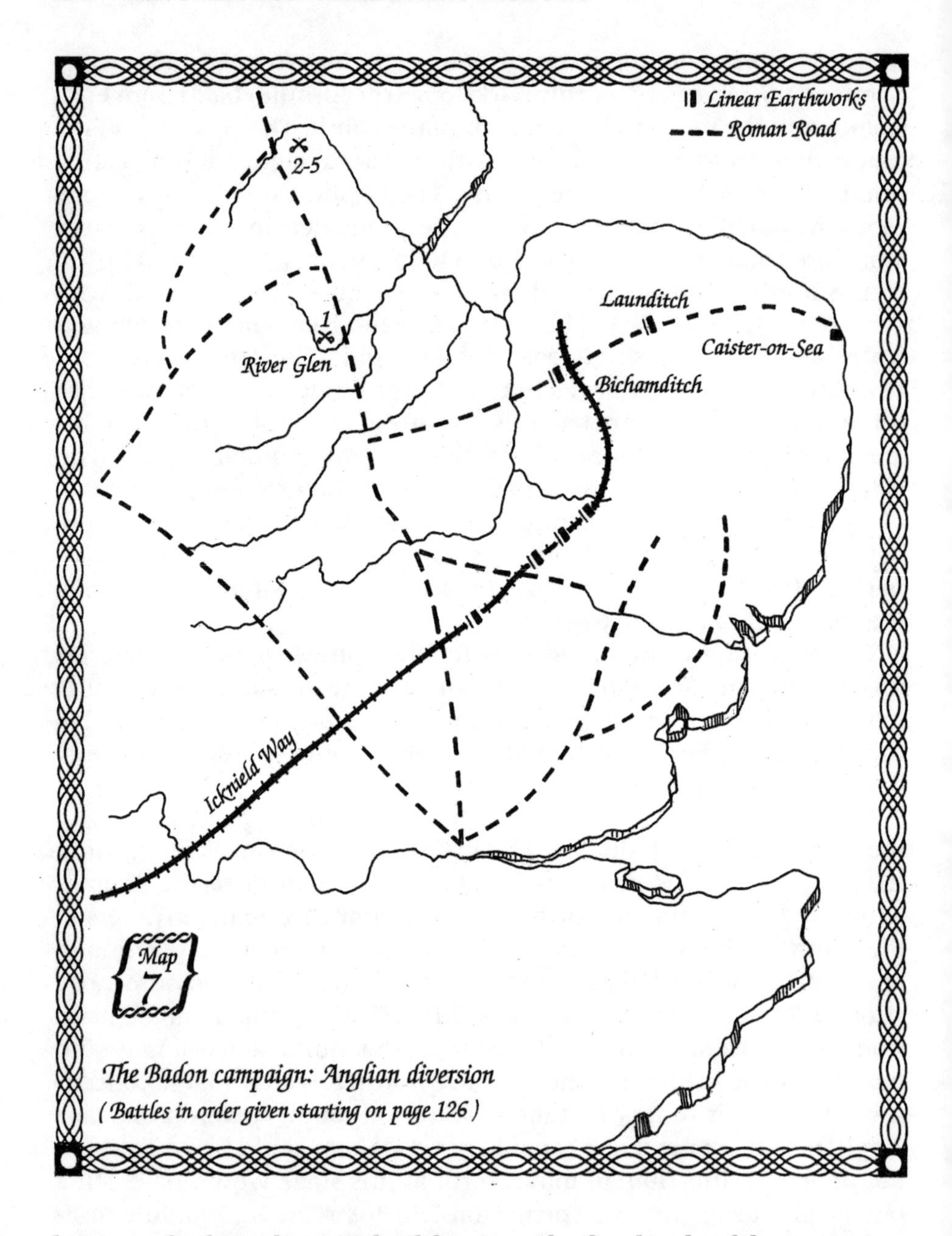


*The Badon campaign: Anglian diversion*
*(Battles in order given starting on page 126)*

here, not far from the mouth of the river, the first battle of the campaign was fought. If so, it was an ideal site for a cavalry engagement where the Anglo-Saxon infantry could be driven back, with the river confining them in the rear and on either side. It was certainly recorded as a victory for Arthur, an auspicious start to the campaign.

After this success Arthur was again faced with a choice. Should he accept the victory as decisive and turn north against the Lincolnshire settlements, or move further into the East Anglian bridgehead in an attempt to invest and destroy the invasion centres of the eastern invaders? Once again, no competent military commander could imagine that the power of the enemy had been completely neutralized after a single encounter. Indeed, after this engagement there is no mention in the text of any great destruction of the enemy, such as took place following the battles at Guinnion Fort and Badon Hill. Under these circumstances, it is almost certain that Arthur would have proceeded further against East Anglia.

A few kilometres south of the River Glen, another Roman road branches eastward from the Lincoln–London road, leading from Peterborough to Caister-on-Sea. Arthur may well have taken this route. If he did he would, after some 64 kilometres (40 miles), have encountered the first of a series of linear earthworks built to defend East Anglia from any potential enemy coming from the west.

The existence of these linear earthworks in East Anglia is important for an understanding of Dark Age history in the region. Some suggestion has been made that they are relics of frontier disputes between the later kingdoms of Mercia and East Anglia, but this does not accord well with the facts of seventh-century history. A more likely hypothesis is that they were constructed at some time in the period under discussion here – that is, in the time of Ambrosius or Arthur. It is possible that the Bichamditch and the Launditch on the Peterborough–Caister-on-Sea road were constructed when Ambrosius had regained control of central Britain and after Hengist and Aesc had been driven back into Kent in the 450s. They were no doubt manned following the battle on the River Glen, when the Angles felt that Arthur could perhaps advance eastwards in order to follow up his victory. (Other linear earthworks further to the south may well have been engineered at the same time, but these are more relevent to matters raised in the next chapter.)

If, as is highly probable, Arthur did in fact attempt to destroy the Anglian bridgeheads of the invaders by an attack along the Caister-on-Sea road, it is very likely that it was here he met with his first reverse. The reason for this lies in the type of force he had chosen for his campaign.

Under the influence of Rome and of his Celtic forebears, he had chosen cavalry, probably light and almost certainly without stirrups. The latter piece of horse equipment originally came from China in the sixth century, via the Slavs of central Asia, and so was not available to Arthur's cavalry in the late fifth century. The absence of the stirrup would not affect cavalry mobility, or the advantage of the cavalry charge over infantry in open country. It would, however, certainly reduce the stability of the mounted cavalryman when attacking a prepared position, such as the perimeter of a fort or the ditch and rampart of a linear earthwork.

If Arthur did indeed move east along the Caister-on-Sea road, he would have encountered the first linear earthwork at Bichamditch. Success here would have been difficult, but if it was achieved, there was a second earthwork 17.5 kilometres (11 miles) further on at Launditch (see Map 7 on page 124). He may have felt that the losses he faced would prejudice his main objective of attacking and defeating the Anglo-Saxons, the Scots and the Irish, wherever they were. There is no evidence that the East Anglian bridgehead was eliminated by Arthur, and it must be assumed that he retreated back to the Lincoln–London road and then resumed his campaign northwards. Needless to say, the bard who wrote the poem from which the paragraph in Nennius was derived would make no mention of any reverse that Arthur may have experienced in Norfolk. Nevertheless, Norfolk and Suffolk were not restored to British control.

In Lincolnshire there are several large early fifth-century cemeteries, more to the south than to the north of Lincoln itself. The southern cemeteries lie within or close to the bow of the River Witham (probably the Dubglas of the Nennius record), which flows north-east from its source until it reaches Lincoln and then turns south-east to end in the Wash. It was the invaders from settlements close to these southern cemeteries who would first have met Arthur as he moved north towards Lincoln and into the bow of the river (see Map 7 on page 124). The lie of the land here would have favoured cavalry action, just as it did on the River Glen, with the additional advantage that there is no evidence of the invaders having built linear earthworks such as those found in East Anglia. It is tempting to identify the River Witham with the Dubglas in the Nennius record and the four battles with the progressive reduction of all the Lincolnshire settlements. Arthur could have achieved success piecemeal by attacking the settlements within the bow first and then tempting those outside the bow to cross the river, where they also could have been defeated. The tactics that proved to be useful on the River Glen could also have been used to advantage on the River Witham in Lincolnshire.

After victory in the four battles in Lincolnshire, Arthur would have been free to continue on his way northwards following the Roman roads. In order to avoid the Humber estuary, he would probably have crossed the Aire near the village of Ledsham, some 16 kilometres (10 miles) east of Leeds. There is no record of any visit to the old headquarters of the Duke of the Britains at York. Consequently, of the two Roman roads leading north in Yorkshire, one on either side of the Vale of York, it is probable that Arthur took the western, which passes through Catterick and does not touch York.

The Anglo-Saxon invasions of Britain from Lincolnshire to Northumberland probably all started from the estuary of the Humber, and those north of that river finally resulted in the establishment of the kingdoms of Deira (in Yorkshire) and Bernicia (beyond the Tees). In the later fifth century, the concentration of the invaders would thus have decreased as the distance northwards from the Humber increased, and consequently the opposition to Arthur from the Anglo-Saxons would have decreased the further north he travelled. Nevertheless, he fought at least one battle on the River Bassas, the sixth in the series, in this region, on one of the many rivers he had to cross before reaching Hadrian's Wall.

There is something else supporting Arthur's possible choice of the western road through Yorkshire. This Roman road is the only one east of Carlisle which crosses Hadrian's Wall and also leads direct to Celidon Wood, located by Skene on the upper reaches of the Tweed. After crossing the Wall, new opponents appeared. In addition to invaders from the Continent, these were most probably enemies from further north, either the Picts from beyond the Forth–Clyde line or, more probably, the Scots from the region between the Wall and the Forth and Clyde rivers. The names of these two tribes indicate their origins. The word Scots derives from the Latin name for the Irish and the word Picts is the Latin name for the tribes north of the Forth and Clyde. The Scots invaded from Ireland and gradually pushed the Picts northwards, and by the ninth century an Irish-Scots dynasty had finally conquered the whole of Pictland. All the land north of Hadrian's Wall took the name of Scotland from that time onwards. Arthur's seventh victory in the Forest of Celidon may well have been against the Scots, the first to be encountered after crossing the Wall (see Map 6 on page 122).

The fact that it was a victory is important in again demonstrating Arthur's military ability. He may have known of Varus's defeat, described in Chapter 3, which clearly showed the tremendous danger faced by cavalry fighting in a forest environment. Understanding the temperamental, undisciplined nature of his opponents, particularly if they were the Celtic Scots, he could rely on luring them out of the forest, perhaps on to the lower slopes of the Cheviots, where he could have taken advantage of the slope in a downhill charge to defeat them.

Alternatively, he could have encountered the enemy on open ground near the Tweed, where the same tactics as were used on the Rivers Glein and Dubglas could be employed. At least the victory here established the Wall as the northern border of Arthur's territory, for this battle marked the most northerly point of the campaign. Control north of the Wall, which the Romans found very difficult if not impossible to achieve, was certainly equally impossible for Arthur.

Following the victory in the Forest of Celidon, Arthur may have encountered another enemy in the same area. The eighth battle at Guinnion Fort (see Map 6 on page 122) was, as suggested by Skene, most likely located in an abandoned Roman fort near Stow-in-Wedale. Wedale lies to the east of Celidon Wood and is therefore closer to the east coast. It was thus more likely at this time to have been occupied by the Anglo-Saxons, the 'heathen' of the Nennius record. Both Celidon Wood and Wedale are close to the Roman road probably used by Arthur after crossing Hadrian's Wall, and Skene's locations for the battles in the wood and at Guinnion Fort are probably accurate. In the latter engagement, the enemy clearly left the fort to meet Arthur in the open, for the record states that they 'were put to flight on that day and there was a great slaughter upon them'.

After Guinnion Fort the ninth battle took place at Chester and to reach this location Arthur's forces had to cross the island to the west coast. After retracing their steps south to Hadrian's Wall along the same road used for the advance north, three Roman roads were available: the first was along Hadrian's Wall to Carlisle and then south to Chester; the second was via Bishop Auckland and Barnard Castle to the Carlisle–Chester road and then south; and the third was across the Pennines by the York–Manchester–Chester road. All three routes were used by the legions.

If Arthur took either of the first two routes, he would have entered the British kingdom of Rheged. Such a visit would have been useful in gaining the support of an important British ally in his attempt to eliminate the Anglo-Saxon threat to Britain. To avoid contact with Rheged by taking the trans-Pennine route via York and Manchester would have meant not only retracing the tracks of his northward journey even further south but also reducing his chances of gaining the support of an important northern kingdom. There is no evidence for an Arthurian battle in Rheged.

It is just possible that the battle at Chester was fought against a small expeditionary force of Anglo-Saxons which had penetrated across the Pennines from the East Riding of Yorkshire. It is far more likely that here the opposition was an Irish force, for much of Wales,

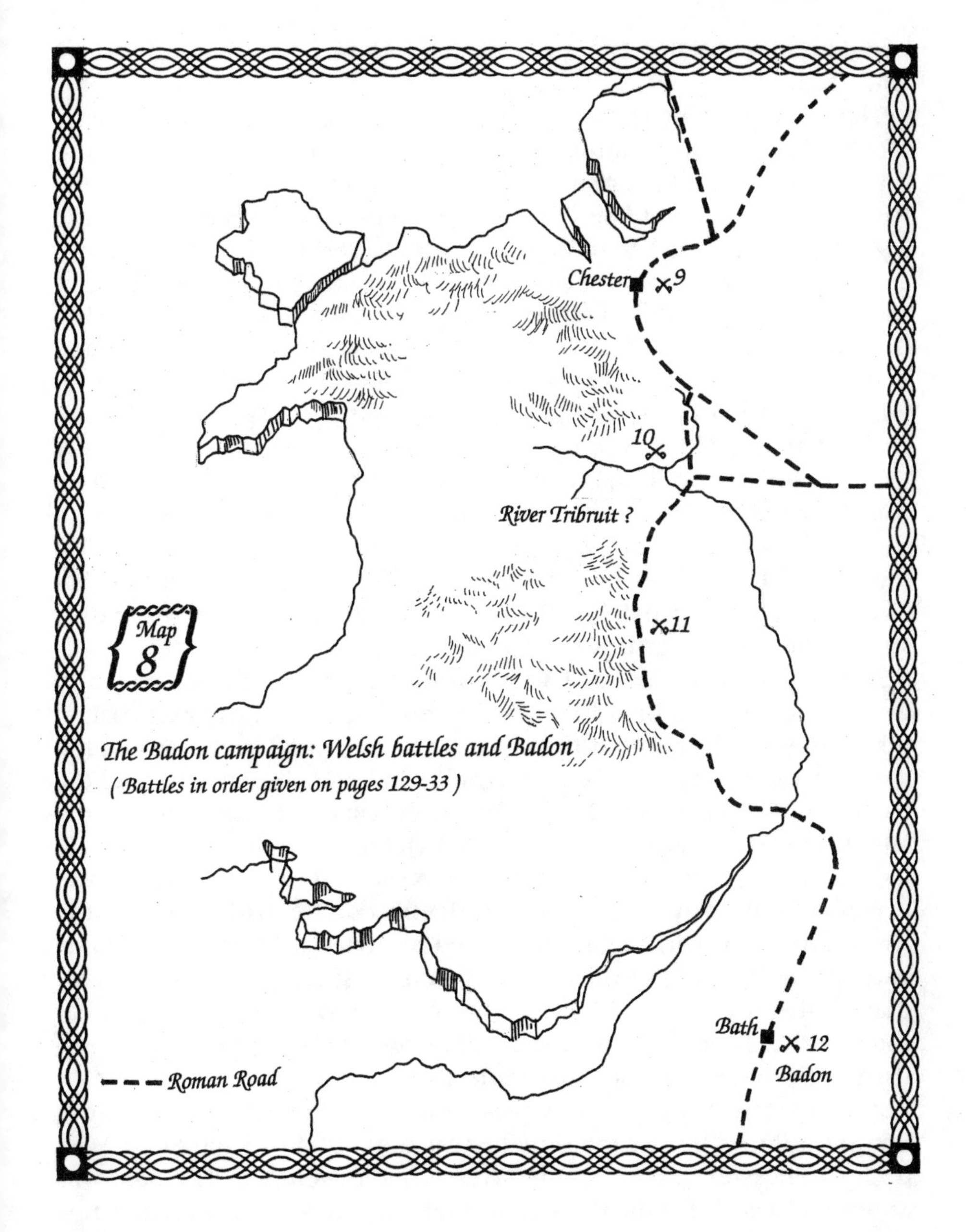


The Badon campaign: Welsh battles and Badon
(Battles in order given on pages 129-33)

both north and south, was colonized by the Irish in the fourth century. The Irish, being Celts, would have been more than willing to leave the comparative safety of the legionary fort to meet Arthur on open ground, as their Celtic temperament demanded (see Map 8 on page 129). Arthur was again victorious and his authority over north Wales secured; indeed, there is a record of a British leader, Catwallaun

Longhand, who later expelled the Irish from both Caernarfonshire and Anglesey.

The tenth and eleventh battles in the series, following the engagement at Chester, were almost certainly also concerned with the recovery of Wales from the Irish. The site of the tenth on the bank of the River Tribruit has not been previously identified. On the basis of the arguments presented here, it should, however, lie between Chester and the eleventh battle at Leintwardine. A Roman road leads directly from Chester through Leintwardine and Hereford to Gloucester, thence rejoining the Fosse Way at Cirencester. Between Chester and Leintwardine, the road crosses the Severn at Wroxeter, at the point where that river is joined by a tributary, the Tern, spelt Tren by the Anglo-Saxons. This could be the site of the tenth battle on the River Tribruit and victory here, together with the success at Leintwardine, could have set the pattern for the ultimate subjugation of the Irish in south Wales (see Map 8 on page 129). Once again, as in north Wales, there is evidence of initial victory by Arthur leading to further British victories by later British generals which finally resulted in the expulsion of the Irish dynasties from Wales.

In his campaign, Arthur had certainly shown the flag successfully over the length and breadth of the island and had clearly established his reputation throughout the land. He had divided and defeated the Angles in Lincolnshire and East Anglia and had similarly treated the Irish in north and south Wales. He had warned the Scots against any attempt to cross Hadrian's Wall by his victories north of the Wall. He had, however, only been partially successful in his strategic plan to invest and destroy the enemy bridgeheads. He had defeated the Angles in open warfare but had failed to penetrate their strongholds and also failed to eject the invaders from East Anglia, very possibly due to the difficulties faced by his cavalry when attacking linear earthworks. There is additionally no record of the Angles in Lincolnshire suffering exceptional casualties.

After Leintwardine, the way was clear for Arthur to return to base at South Cadbury, but by the time he was moving down the Fosse Way from Cirencester to Bath another threat had developed. The date was around 496 and it will be recalled that, according to *The Anglo-Saxon Chronicle,* Aelle in 490 had besieged and captured the town of Andred near the site of Pevensey on the south coast. Between 490 and 496 Aelle would no doubt have heard of Arthur's victorious campaign and possibly of the death of Ambrosius, the High King. As a consequence, he may well have decided to intercept Arthur on his way back to South Cadbury and destroy the new British leader, perhaps taking advantage of British battle fatigue after a long campaign.

The reasons for taking such a decision could very possibly have arisen from the position of authority that Aelle had reached in the 19 years since his arrival in Britain in 477. According to Bede, he was the first Bretwalda and, to reach this eminence, he must have established some sort of control over the invaders in the south of the island. In particular, he was certainly senior to Aesc, who had only recently (in 488) inherited the leadership of the Kentish invaders from his father, Hengist. Aelle no doubt felt his position challenged by this new leader of the British. He would know that Arthur was completing his successful campaign on the borders of Wales and would probably return to South Cadbury along the Fosse Way. He therefore collected his forces together and marched north-west to meet the enemy directly, fairly confident that any threat to his left flank would be much reduced by Ambrosius's death.

The confrontation on Badon Hill has been confirmed from three sources: Gildas's book, the *Annales Cambriae* and Nennius's *History*. Gildas describes the battle as a siege which ended in a conclusive British victory. The length of the siege is confirmed in the *Annales Cambriae,* which describe a three-day engagement. Nennius's *History* emphasizes the numbers of Anglo-Saxons slaughtered, almost 1,000, although this number, 'three times three hundred and three score', and the allocation of all the deaths to Arthur personally, are both probable examples of poetic licence. It would be almost certain that Arthur placed his cavalry on the high ground and used the cavalry charge repeatedly downhill to cause the maximum damage to the Anglo-Saxons. The three-day engagement described in the *Annales Cambriae* would have required Arthur to camp on the hill and this in turn would fit with the description of the battle as a siege by Gildas.

The defeat at Badon probably effectively ended Aelle's tenure as Bretwalda. Arthur's victory here, and in all the other engagements of the campaign collectively referred to here as the Badon campaign, is all the more remarkable when the nature of the command he exercised is compared with that exercised by the leaders of the invaders. Although Arthur may have wished to restore a Roman Britain, there had been a reversion to Celtic customs under Vortigern. As explained in Chapter 2, the nature of Celtic kingship is very circumscribed by limitations in the king's authority and, additionally, Celtic tribal loyalty could easily override loyalty to the national cause. Arthur's success was achieved in spite of these problems.

No such problems were faced by the Anglo-Saxons. Their kings and

Bretwaldas held supreme authority without the limitations placed upon their Celtic opposite numbers. They were elected, usually from members of the royal house, but after election could not be deposed. When Aelle became Bretwalda – the ruler of Britain – he could, in time of war, call the subject kings to his standard to fight under his leadership. If this happened at Badon, then the nature of Arthur's victory is again enhanced.

At the end of the campaign, Arthur had reinforced and extended the control over central Britain that Vortimer and, more particularly, Ambrosius had wrested from the invaders after the first surge westwards between 440 and 446. He was, however, more successful in the north and west than he was in the east. The Scots were to remain thereafter behind the Wall. The Irish were to surrender dynastic control of Wales to the British, although some Irish immigrants remained and were absorbed into the local population. In the east, the state of affairs was somewhat different.

After Badon there is no record of any Anglo-Saxon victory, other than coastal affrays and the capture of the Isle of Wight, until the battle of Salisbury in 552. The twelfth battle of the campaign was the most decisive one of all and it set the scene for the relative peace that was reported by Gildas which had certainly lasted up until his time of writing – around 540.

The whole campaign was a major factor in delaying the Anglo-Saxon conquest by almost 100 years. As a consequence, there is some justification in regarding the Badon campaign as the most successful of Arthur's military achievements. Nevertheless, the campaign did not, in spite of the total absence of any recorded defeats, fulfil all of Arthur's strategic objectives. The second target had not been achieved: Arthur had not invested and destroyed the enemy bridgeheads in East Anglia and Kent, or any of the smaller bridgeheads along the south coast. It is also very possible that the victories in Lincolnshire were by no means total. The difficulties faced by the British cavalry and their limitations necessitated a change of strategy, and this is the subject of the next chapter.

# The East Anglian Campaign

THE DEFEAT of the Anglo-Saxons at Badon Hill halted the invasion in the south, except possibly for minor coastal activity, and the pause lasted for some 50 years. The evidence for this is clearly provided in *The Anglo-Saxon Chronicle*. The South Saxons, under Aelle's direct rule, were the most affected, since they probably played the greatest part in the invaders' initiative against Arthur at Badon, following the near completion of his campaign down the west side of the island. Thereafter, evidence both of Aelle as Bretwalda and of South Saxon activity disappears from *The Anglo-Saxon Chronicle* during the rest of the conquest of Britain.

Other invasion bridgeheads in both south and east were equally static. The West Saxon invasion, which started at about the same time as the battle at Badon Hill, did not reach Charford, only about 30 kilometres (18 miles) from the coast, until 519 and even then the *Chronicle* does not report positive victory. The conquest of the Isle of Wight by the West Saxons was not accomplished until 530, and real progress into the centre of Britain was not achieved until after the victory at Salisbury in 552.

The Kentish kingdom after 488 was ruled by Aesc, the son of Hengist, and was bounded to the north by the south bank of the Thames estuary and on the west by some of the Ambrosian recruitment sites. No revival of aggression in Kent was recorded until 568, when Ceawlin stemmed the first signs of a Kentish western offensive led by Aethelbert. There was, equally, still no sign of any aggressive action on the part of the Angles in East Anglia or Lincolnshire.

In the west of Britain, victories had been gained by Arthur at Chester, Leintwardine and on the River Tribruit, followed by successful action taken by Catwallaun Longhand in north Wales and by

Agricola in Demetia (south Wales) to eliminate danger from the leaders of the Irish immigrants.

The south and west of Britain had clearly reverted to near stability after Badon, with adequate containment of the southern, eastern and western invaders. This conclusion is supported by Gildas, who states in about 540 that, after Ambrosius's intervention: 'From then on victory went now to our countrymen, now to their enemies ... This lasted right up to the year of the siege of Badon Hill, pretty well the last defeat of the villains, and certainly not the least.' The reference to 'pretty well the last defeat' suggests that, in the 44 years between Badon and the date of Gildas's book, there was no substantial advance of the invaders. It is unlikely that news of their progress, if it had occurred, would not have reached Gildas, even if he was writing at some location in the West Country.

In spite of these indications of a long pause in the Anglo-Saxon invasion sequence, there is no documentary record of any British initiative against their Anglo-Saxon enemies from the time of Badon in 496 up to the battle of Camlann in 517, when Arthur died. It is most unlikely that, during this period, Arthur would have been able to afford to rest on the laurels he had gained in the Badon campaign and even more unlikely that he did so. Yet if he had undertaken a victorious campaign comparable with his first, it certainly would have been remembered by the bards. The need for further action by Arthur to extend the pause has to be reconciled with the lack of bardic records of victory. This need is met and reconciliation achieved by the suggested East Anglian campaign described below.

After the largely successful campaign which ended at Badon, Arthur may have felt that he had partially restored a Roman state similar to that achieved by Aegidius and Syagrius and, in contrast to the latter, that he had effectively contained the invader within their original bridgeheads. There is, however, no record of any Arthurian activity north of the Humber–Mersey line after the Badon victory and it is very probable that, in spite of the victories on the River Bassas, in Celidon Wood and at Guinnion Fort, Arthur realized that distance and poor communications made it virtually impossible to retain effective control north of the Humber. In any case, there was a British kingdom in this region, Rheged, and opposition to the Anglo-Saxons in the north was probably left to Rheged to organize. Nevertheless, the centre and west of Britain south of the Humber remained substantially under Arthur's control and, after the great efforts of the last half-century, the population here was still largely Romano-Celtic – that is to say, British. The limitations to Arthur's success, however, could not be overlooked.

The series of victories from beyond Hadrian's Wall almost to the south coast of Britain, the elimination of the threat from Aelle, the death of Hengist and the lack of progress of the West Saxons had still left at least two of the bridgeheads posing an unacceptable threat. The most threatening bridgehead, from the Wash as far south as Woodbridge, had resisted Arthur's best attempts to invest and destroy it very early in his campaign and he may even have been doubtful of complete success in the more northerly bridgehead in Lincolnshire. The four battles on the River Dubglas showed the extent and difficulties of the problem facing Arthur in this area. He had failed to eject the Anglo-Saxons from Britain.

In addition, Britain was no longer as prosperous as it had been under imperial authority, the Roman villas and estates had suffered irreversible damage under the stress of civil war and invasion and, as Gildas reports, the cities had been destroyed and had not been rebuilt. The long lines of communication between South Cadbury and the rest of Britain meant that the degree of control that Arthur, as High King, exercised over the increasingly Celtic petty kings of Britain was open to question.

In parenthesis, it is these petty kings who became the knights of the Round Table in the romantic legends written some 600 years later. Indeed, some of the names of the knights can be linked with the names of local kings in earlier times. Sir Percival, for example, takes his name from Peredur of York, who died in 580, and Sir Tristan derives from Tristan, King of Cornwall, who lived in Castle Dore almost 100 years after Arthur's time. Other knights – for example, Sir Lancelot and Sir Galahad – are pure literary inventions. However, the legendary King Arthur exercised very little control over his knights and this no doubt mirrored the real difficulties the High King experienced in holding the minor Celtic kings together in the times of relative peace that followed Badon.

Whatever the difficulties that Arthur faced in gaining the support of the petty kings of Britain, he surely realized that such problems could, in some measure, always be diminished by an external threat to the Celtic nation. The continued danger of invasion from the two eastern bridgeheads could have supplied the threat which would have enabled Arthur to gain widespread Celtic support for a second major campaign to eject the invaders from these, their two strongest, bridgeheads. This campaign would also, hopefully, restrain or even terminate the invasion of Britain if it were successful.

There is no direct documentary evidence for this second campaign, in contrast with the bardic poem which celebrated the successes of Arthur's first campaign, which ended in the great victory of Badon. This is not surprising, as it resulted in no victories comparable with those of the first campaign. However, in spite of the lack of direct evidence and the absence of specific victories, there is indirect evidence supporting the probability of a second campaign and much of this follows from Arthur's innate abilities as a strategist. The threat from the east would have been very likely to make Arthur consider the available options in order to counter the threat. In order to develop the concept of a second campaign even further, a likely course of action will be suggested which Arthur may well have planned. The various stages of the campaign can be supported by evidence to make each step a reasonable development of the hypothesis.

The status of the eastern settlements must have been well known to Arthur. They were the furthest from South Cadbury of all the Anglo-Saxon bridgeheads south of the Humber and they consequently presented a continuing threat to the centre of Britain. The most substantial settlement of the two was in East Anglia, bounded by the Great Ouse and the River Deben, but there were also large settlements in Lincolnshire. Apart from these two centres of Anglian strength, the rest of Britain south of the Humber posed, as indicated earlier, little cause for immediate concern for the High King.

Faced with this situation of limited success but nevertheless encouraged by the decisive victory at Badon, Arthur may well have felt that a second campaign had to be planned in order to protect the heartland of Britain, the lands south of a line joining the Humber to the Mersey, from the two Anglian settlements in the east.

To the south of the Humber–Mersey line, the East Anglian bridgehead presented an even greater threat to the British than did the Lincolnshire settlements, since the former was closer to London and the latter had been subdued in the Badon campaign. In contrast to this subjection, there is no record of the invaders in East Anglia ever being defeated, nor had they ever been displaced since their first arrival in the early years of the fifth century. Consequently, taking advantage of the fact that the south and the south-east of the island were comparatively quiescent, Arthur would have been likely to direct his second campaign towards the destruction of the East Anglian bridgehead, the scene of his suggested failure in the earlier Badon campaign.

This time it is possible that he took a different and more direct route towards his target, avoiding the scene of possible earlier defeats in north Norfolk. A second useful line of communication from South

Cadbury to the east was provided by the Icknield Way, a pre-Roman ridgeway leading from the Fosse Way, at a point near Bath, eastwards to the Chilterns and then north-east along the line of those hills towards East Anglia. Arthur could have joined the nearest Roman road some eight kilometres (five miles) north of South Cadbury and then proceeded east to Silchester to join the Icknield Way at the Goring Gap in the Chilterns. This route lay to the south of the Fosse Way and provided a more direct access to the centre of the Anglian region than did the Roman road used in the earlier campaign, where, it will be remembered, the intention was to divide the Lincolnshire from the East Anglian bridgeheads.

However, the use of the Icknield Way for the second foray against the East Anglian invaders would have led to the same type of obstacle as may have been encountered on the first campaign. There is a series of linear earthworks at right angles to the Icknield Way as the ridge-way passes south of Cambridge. As in the case of the earthworks on the Caistor-on-Sea road, the Icknield earthworks face in a direction to defend the east from an attack coming from the south-west. There are four such defensive lines crossing the Icknield Way: these are, successively from the south, Heydon Ditch, Flean Ditch, Devil's Ditch and the Black Ditches (see Map 9 on page 138). Clearly, the Angles respected the military abilities of the British forces led by Arthur and the defensive barriers would have been manned as Arthur approached. The earthworks were probably constructed, as were those in Norfolk, by the Angles or perhaps even earlier.

British cavalry advancing northward up the Icknield Way from South Cadbury to make a second attempt at reducing the Anglian bridgehead would have found the task just as difficult as they may have found it in Norfolk in the initial stages of the earlier campaign. Once again, there is no evidence of any Arthurian military success in East Anglia after Badon. If there was a second attempt to penetrate the Anglo-Saxon Anglian defences, there was certainly a second failure, although, as will be indicated later, some progress may have been made in an attack directed northwards up the Icknield Way which overcame the first three linear earthworks but was finally held at the Black Ditches defence line, just south of the River Lark.

This probable second failure must have ended any hope Arthur may have had of expelling the invaders from their eastern bridgeheads. Nevertheless, something had to be done to maintain the morale of the British. Lacking military success when facing the obstinate resistance presented by the Anglian warriors manning the linear earthworks, the only available alternative would have been to concentrate on the

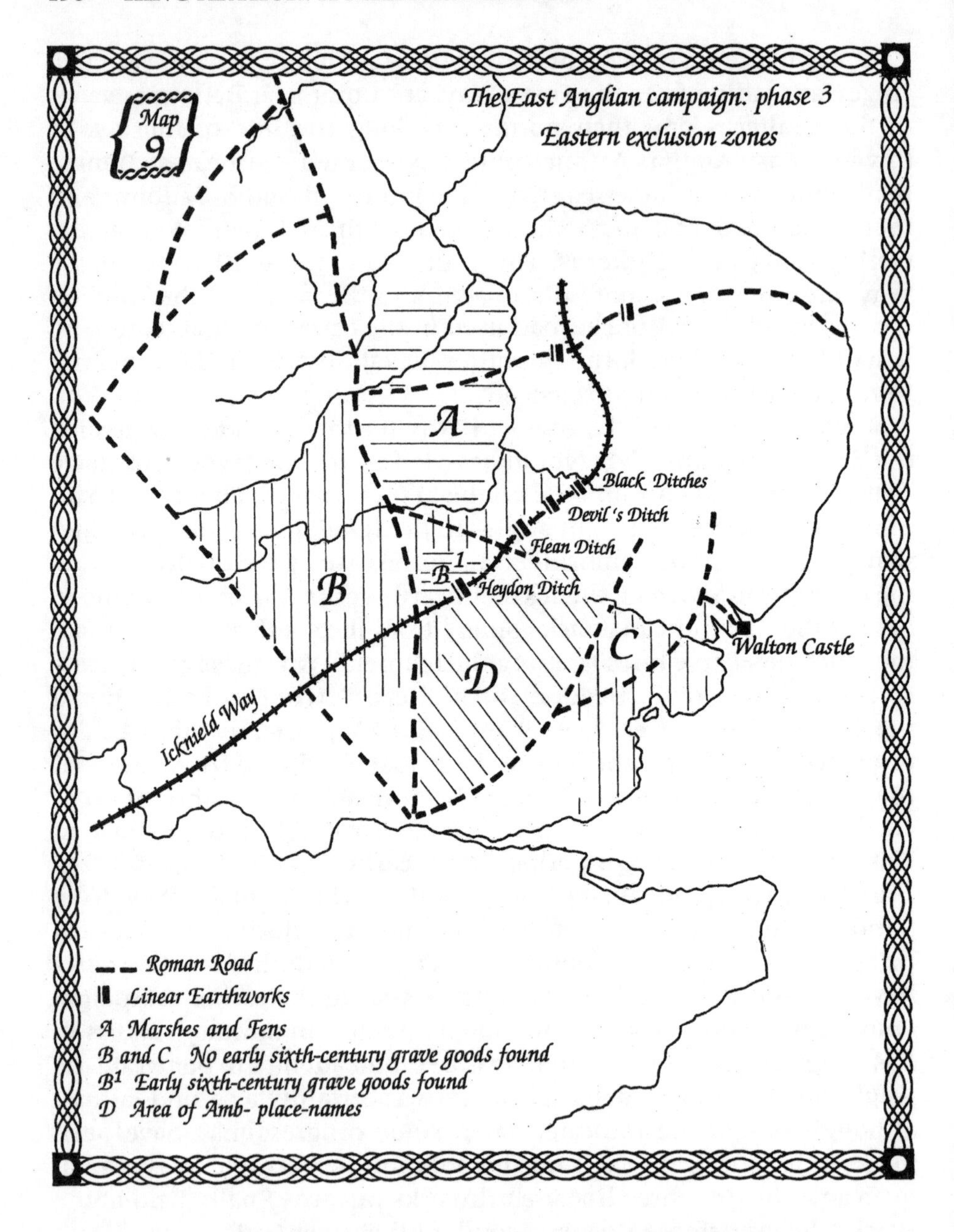


containment of the threat. This policy, if successful, would have had the added advantage of allowing a period for much-needed British recovery after the destruction and instability caused by the invaders, and after the nationwide exhaustion following the long Badon campaign and the second attempt to reduce the eastern bridgeheads.

If a containment decision was taken, it had to be applied to both the

East Anglian and the Lincolnshire settlements in a more deliberate and direct manner than may have been considered necessary in earlier days. Any policy of containment would need to impose some sort of barrier to separate these bridgeheads and to divide them both from the rest of Britain. A physical barrier based on geographical features, such as a river or a range of hills or an area of marshland, would be most helpful.

In the case of the most northerly of the bridgeheads in Lincolnshire, the earlier campaign battles on the River Dubglas in Lincolnshire were probably not decisive. Even so, the Badon campaign had placed a western limit to the expansion of this settlement on the River Trent. A southern limit was formed by the upper reaches of the River Nene and by the Fens. On this basis, little further action was required by Arthur in order to achieve adequate containment of the more distant Lincolnshire settlements and their separation from the nearer and more southerly invaders in East Anglia.

The Fens, however, were the only natural barrier available to confine the East Anglian bridgehead and their location made them inadequate to restrain an active and resourceful invader from advancing aggressively in a south-westerly direction. Since direct attack had failed, something more was required. A complete solution to the problem would require an additional barrier between the East Anglian bridgehead and the rest of Britain, including the Kentish kingdom south of the Thames.

Valuable information relating to the development of some form of barrier in these areas has been provided by Dr Morris in his book *The Age of Arthur* (1973:136). He has suggested that a form of barrier can be deduced from the archaeological records at cemetery locations round the southern limits of the Lincolnshire bridgehead and the western and south-western limits of the East Anglian bridgehead. In order to relate his suggestions to the theme of Arthur's containment activities in East Anglia, the barrier areas can be specifically defined.

The most northerly boundary of the East Anglian bridgehead bordering south Lincolnshire was formed, first, of a stretch of land around the Wash which was clear of all Anglo-Saxon cemeteries and probably almost clear of any inhabitants due to the marshes and fens which predominate in that part of the country (see Map 9 on page 138: area A). Adjacent to this was a further band, about 48 kilometres (30 miles) wide, linking the southern edge of the Lincolnshire bridgehead on the upper reaches of the Nene with the boundary of the East Anglian bridgehead on the River Lark. Within this band, Morris notes that in the Anglo-Saxon cemeteries there are grave goods which show 'much of the fifth century, much of the late sixth, nothing of the early sixth' (see Map 9 on page 138: area B). There is an abundance of early sixth-century grave goods elsewhere, but their absence here is noteworthy.

There is a small area inside this band, some eight kilometres (five miles) south-west of Cambridge, where early sixth-century grave goods are not excluded (see Map 9 on page 138: area B[1]). Here Morris suggests that the invaders were allowed to remain, possibly as allies of the British. Similar small Anglo-Saxon settlements on the Upper Thames and elsewhere posed little danger to Arthur.

A southerly inter-bridgehead area (see Map 9 on page 138: area C) separates East Anglia from Kent and also protects the coast from the Thames to the Orwell from further invasion. The area lies between these two rivers and stretches eastwards from the Roman road linking London with Norfolk via Bury St Edmunds and Ixworth, as far as the Essex coast. In this area also Morris notes that there is no clear evidence of early sixth-century grave goods.

It would appear that, in the early sixth century, after the end of Arthur's great Badon campaign, in critical areas previously held by Anglo-Saxons the invaders were excluded and what were effectively containment barriers or exclusion zones were created. It would not be necessary for the British to take any particular action to link the two exclusion zones B and C, for the area between them coincides with the line of Ambrosian recruitment centres to the north-east of London, an area which was probably firmly held by the British during the three last decades of the fifth century (see Map 9 on page 138: area D).

As argued earlier, the necessity for a barrier lay in the failure of the 'invest and destroy' element of Arthur's strategic plan in his Badon campaign and in the secondary campaign after Badon. It is consequently necessary to consider how the barrier could have been created and maintained, for Arthur's post-Badon plans were important factors in deferring the final victory of the Anglo-Saxons for a period much longer than it took Clovis and the Franks to achieve final victory in Gaul.

It is probable that the expulsion of the Anglo-Saxons from the two critical areas began immediately after the abortive second attempt to break into the East Anglian bridgehead by British forces advancing up the Icknield Way at some time in the last few years of the fifth century or early years of the sixth. The eastern edge of the most northerly exclusion zone coincides roughly with the line of the River Lark and includes the point near the Lark where the Black Ditches linear earthwork crosses the Icknield Way. It would therefore seem that in his Icknield offensive Arthur managed to overrun the Heydon, Flean and Devil's Ditches but was held on the River Lark and Black Ditches line. At this point, having once again failed to penetrate beyond the Lark into the major East Anglian settlements, he may well have moved westwards and cleared the northern zone (see Map 9: area B on page 138) of any remaining Anglo-Saxon settlements as far as the upper reaches of the River Nene. Leaving some part of his force behind to police the zone and to hold the line against any incursions from the Anglian settlements in Lincolnshire, he could then have moved south-east through the Ambrosian recruitment sites as far as the Essex coast, clearing area C (see Map 9 on page 138) between the River Deben and the Thames estuary of the invaders' settlements, probably East Saxon.

At this stage it would have been possible for Arthur to command an area stretching from the coast of Essex to the River Nene which was clear of any invaders, except those who were his allies near Cambridge. It would have been quite impossible for him to deploy either the power or resources which would have been needed to construct a defensive linear earthwork in the east comparable to that built in the west on the borders of Wales by Offa in the last years of the eighth century. Even so Arthur's concept of containment was similar to that of Offa, or closer still to the idea behind the Welsh Marches, a defended frontier between England and Wales established by the Normans some seven centuries after Arthur.

The next problem facing Arthur was that of setting up an organization capable of holding the East Anglian Marches and using it to inhibit any thrust westwards or south-westwards from the main concentrations of Angles in Norfolk and Suffolk, or any thrust southwards from the Lincolnshire settlements. He could not devote his own time exclusively to the task, for as High King his responsibility was, nominally, to the whole of Britain, from Hadrian's Wall to the south coast, together with all the land as far as the western seaboard. In fact, actual control exercised by the High King probably diminished, or even ceased, at the Humber–Mersey line.

The difficulties to be faced in setting up an organization to hold the barrier round the East Anglian settlements were compounded by the fact that, during the long campaigns before and after Badon, strains may have developed in the association of British tribal kings. Even the most enthusiastic must have wearied after almost continual war over three generations – the fathers of Arthur's commanders probably served under Ambrosius and their grandfathers under Vortigern or the Elder Ambrosius.

In addition, although Arthur may have hoped to restore a semi-Roman state following the pattern set by Aegidius, the Celtic nature of the British population had progressively re-emerged throughout the fifth century. Consequently, some of the characteristics of Celtic society had reappeared. As mentioned in Chapter 2, when attacks diminished progressively from sources outside the nation, the Celts were less and less inclined to unite under any supra-tribal leader such as a High King and more inclined to fragmentation under their own tribal chiefs or petty kings. Arthur must have realized this tendency and the consequent need for as strong a control from the centre as could be achieved. It would not be wise for the High King to be continually engaged on the periphery.

If he returned to his headquarters at South Cadbury, he would be in a far better position to control west and central Britain, using the excellent road system radiating from the south-west. He would also be much closer to any danger points which might develop on the south coast. The special problems of the East Anglian bridgehead and its containment could well be devolved under a subordinate commander, with full power to deal with all matters relating to that area. There is some evidence that Arthur did devolve his responsibilities in the east to a 'viceroy'.

Of all the knights in King Arthur's court mentioned in the medieval romances, there is only one who appears in the documentary evidence for the historical Arthur. This mention appears in the *Annales Cambriae* under the date 537 and has been quoted in Chapter 7. The entry records the death of Arthur and Medraut at the battle of Camlann. (As previously explained, the date of 537 in the *Annales* is 21 years later than the date of 516 assigned to Badon in the same annals. If the better date of 496 is adopted for Badon, then Camlann is also better dated in the year 517.) The new name is Medraut, who appears under this name or as Sir Mordred in much of the romantic Arthurian literature of medieval times.

The only other record of the name Medraut in this period is a genealogical entry in *The Book of Saints* which reads 'Dyfnauc Sant m Medraut' or 'Saint Dyfnauc son of Medraut'. According to Morris, Dyfnauc or Domnoc is a common name, but the only sixth- or seventh-century Domnoc known to Britain is the man who named Dunwich in Suffolk. Consequently, Morris concludes that Medraut belonged to a southern dynasty, probably the local king, owing to the link between his son and Suffolk. However, since sons have a strong tendency to live near their father's home, it would be quite reasonable to place both father and son in Suffolk. In that case, Medraut would be a very satisfactory choice for the difficult task of confining the Anglo-Saxons within their eastern bridgehead through British occupation or control of the exclusion zones.

This arrangement would have left Arthur free to concentrate on the even more difficult task of coordinating the defence of the whole country. It would be Medraut's task to police the arc stretching from the coast of Essex to the River Nene, the area from which the invaders had been excluded as a result of the suggested Arthurian campaign after Badon.

Supporting evidence for this hypothesis is needed and some can be found in considering the location of Medraut's home base. As a king or leader in Suffolk around the year 500, he would almost certainly favour a well-defended site for his headquarters. The Roman villas were in decline long before this time and most had disappeared during the fifth century. In any case, they were not usually designed as strongholds and would have been rejected by British military leaders in favour of hill-fort sites such as that at South Cadbury. Medraut would certainly have appreciated the advantages of Arthur's headquarters but would also have known that there were only a few hill-forts to be found in East Anglia. However, there is one other location which would have had an even greater appeal in those rather troubled times.

This other most favoured location was the result of Roman development in the last quarter of the third century, when German tribes started raiding the outskirts of the western Roman Empire. Since the British fleet, the *classis Britannica*, had ceased to function adequately by the end of the second century, the Roman reply to these raids was to build a series of forts on the coast facing the North Sea and the Channel. By the time of the *Notitia Dignitatum*, as indicated in Chapter 3, these were under the command of the Count of the Saxon Shore, but by Arthur's time most had either fallen out of use or been overrun by the invaders.

There were nine forts in all, two of which, at Walton and Burgh, are of interest here. Stephen Johnson identifies Walton Castle with the Portus Adurnai listed as one of the forts of the Saxon Shore in the *Notitia Dignitatum*: a medieval copy shows the insignia of the Count of the Saxon Shore which includes the Portus Adurnai as one of the nine forts. This castle was engulfed by the sea in the eighteenth century but a seventeenth-century drawing exists. Burgh Castle (Gariannonum) lies on the northern boundary of Suffolk and parts of the walls are still

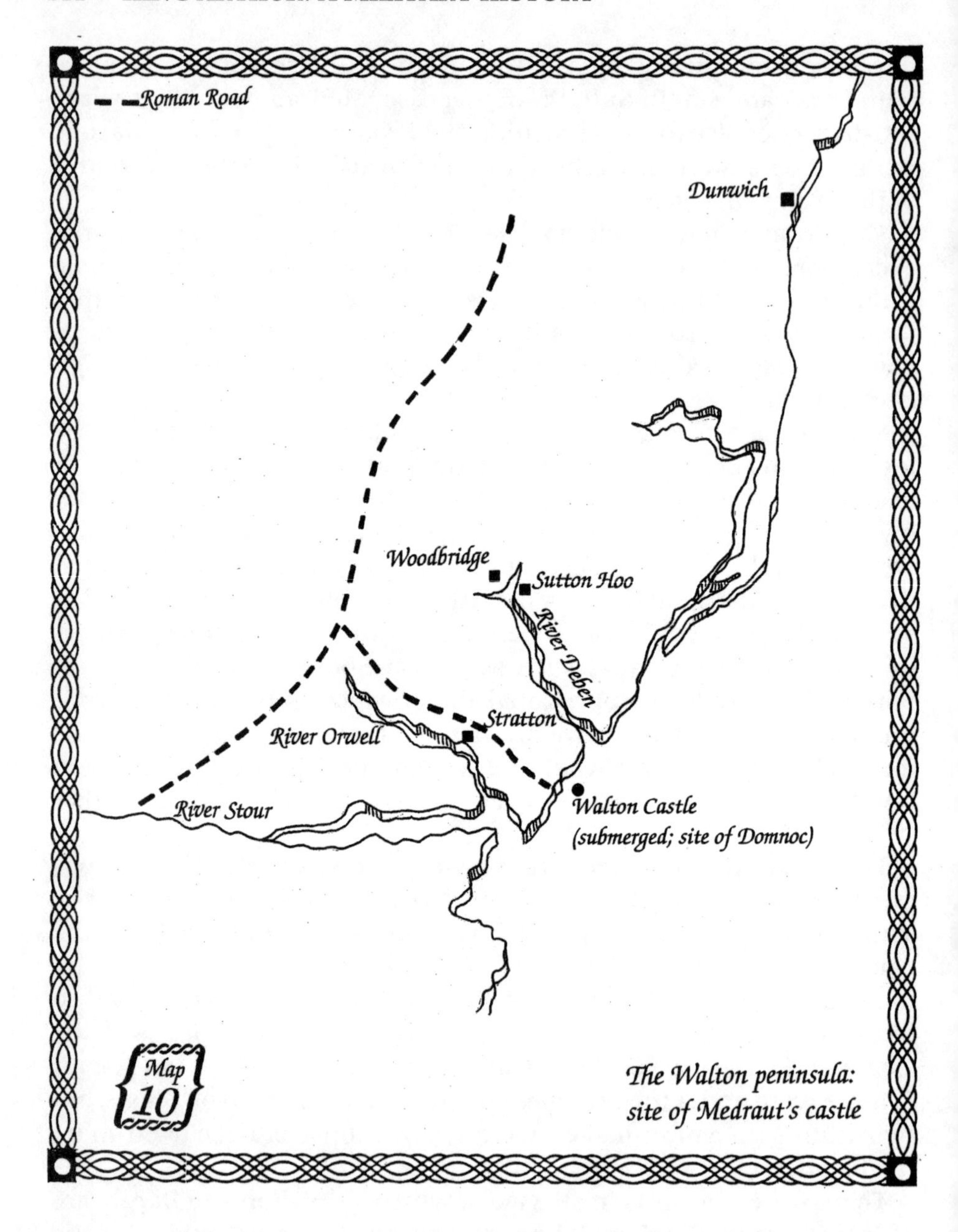


The Walton peninsula: site of Medraut's castle

standing. Both castles would have provided a far better headquarters for Medraut than any hill-fort, but Burgh is too far inside the invaders' bridgehead to have been retained by the British in the year 500. In military terms, Walton Castle at the southern extremity of the exclusion zone would have provided an ideal place for Medraut's home and headquarters (see Map 10 on page 144).

There are other arguments which also provide support for this conclusion. The first of these lies in the origins of the Anglo-Saxon word Walton. The final syllable, 'ton', comes from the Anglo-Saxon *tun,* a village or settlement. There are, according to P. H. Reaney, four different possible derivations for the first syllable: *weala,* foreigner (i.e. British); *weall,* wall; *waelle,* spring or stream; and *weald,* forest. For Walton in Suffolk the first two are equally possible: it could be 'the British settlement' (because it was Medraut's headquarters) or 'the settlement with the wall' (because there was a fort there). The other arguments supporting Medraut's occupation lend further weight to the *weala* derivation.

Another argument which supports Medraut's occupation of Walton Castle follows from recent research relating to the location of Domnoc. In 1961 S. E. Rigold argued in a research paper that Domnoc is not located at Dunwich (as claimed by most authorities and by Morris) but rather at Walton Castle. Such a claim would mean that St Dyfnauc, the son of Medraut, was associated with Walton Castle and not with Dunwich. Consequently, Rigold's argument would provide strong support for the location of Medraut's home and headquarters at Walton Castle.

Rigold's argument is important to the Medraut hypothesis and is summarized here. It was based first on the records of the place-names allocated to the earliest bishop's see in East Anglia. According to Bede, King Sigbert, the son of Raedwald, the fourth Bretwalda, brought Bishop Felix to East Anglia, where his see was established at 'Dommoc' in 627. In *The Anglo-Saxon Chronicle* for the year 798, the name of the see is given as 'Domuce'. In an act of the Council of Clovesho of 803, the name is rendered 'Dummucae' and, finally, in a document dated before 870, the name is quoted as 'Dommuciae'. The consensus of these four primary sources shows, according to Rigold, the true name of the see to be Dommoc, Dommuc or Dummuc. None of these has the Old English '*–wyck*' ending, but all probably have a Romano-British derivation.

William of Malmesbury names the place five times and supports the Romano-British form on each occasion. This is the consensus of all the early manuscripts save one, the late twelfth-century Harl. 3,641, and in this 'Donewyk' replaces 'Dommuc' in a single place. This could be an error by an early scribe, for it is unsupported by any other contemporary evidence.

Florence of Worcester, Gervase, Roger of Wendover and Matthew Paris all use forms close to Dommoc but nothing suggestive of Dunwich. In the fourteenth century, manuscripts of Higden's *Polychronicon* agree on 'Donmic', but in Caxton's printed edition of Trevisa's translation of Higden's work for the first time there appears 'Donwyck', which is clearly intended for Dunwich. Thomas of Elmham had also chosen 'Donwiche' as the name of the see 50 years earlier, perhaps following the single Malmesbury error. Thomas's view is the one taken later by Leland and Camden.

These arguments convince Rigold that the site of the first see was probably not Dunwich. A final piece of evidence enables him to suggest the correct location of Dommoc. This is provided by a text of Bartholomew Cotton, who ends his chronicle in 1298 with a list of bishops of the original see of the East Angles at Dommoc. After using the phrase *'in civitate Donmoc'*, he adds, *'quae nunc Filchestowe vocatur, super mare in orientali parte Suthfolchiae'*. Rigold concludes that what Cotton meant by *'in civitate Donmoc'* was Walton Castle, since that phrase was followed by the statement 'which is now called Felixstowe, on the sea in the eastern part of Suffolk', and the site of the castle was, before inundation, close to Felixstowe. In conclusion, Rigold suggests that, on the most complete plan of Walton Castle, a small ruin in the corner of the enclosure could have been part of the Cathedral of Dommoc.

Some 13 years later Rigold felt that his arguments had not been universally accepted. The late Professor Dorothy Whitelock gave as much emphasis to the Dunwich location of the first see as she did to Rigold's claim for Walton Castle (Whitelock 1972: 1–24). As a result, Rigold developed his thesis further in a later paper in 1974. He there admits that if the variant in Harl. 3,641 is admissible, and not a lapse by a twelfth-century copyist, then Dunwich is the 'tenant in possession'. If not, then the Cotton statement in 1298 has priority and Dunwich loses its 'positive prescription' as the site of the first see in favour of Walton Castle. Following this, he presents three additional arguments which render the case for Dunwich even more precarious. He states:

> (a) that the written claims for Felixstowe are considerably older than 1298 and arguably older that Harl. 3,641;
> (b) that a motive may be suggested for Thomas of Elmham's insistence on Dunwich;
> and (c) that the unhoped-for has come to light two centuries after the archaeological record might have seemed closed – a seventh-century find that would suggest that Walton Castle was at least occupied in the days of Felix.

All this evidence suggests that St Dyfnauc (a name closer to Dommoc than to Domwyck) named Dommoc, which may be identified with Walton Castle. In consequence Medraut, his father, lived in the castle and also used it as his headquarters.

Here Medraut would undoubtedly have been in a very favourable position to maintain the Marches stretching westwards from the Essex coast in a band between 48 and 64 kilometres (30 and 40 miles) wide as far north as the River Nene. His base at Walton, on the southern edge of the East Anglian bridgehead, was secure and would have enabled a close watch to be kept on the invasion coast to both the north and the south.

Additionally, westward communication would have been excellent. There was almost certainly a Roman road leading west from Walton through the village of Stratton (see Map 10 on page 144) to join the main Colchester–Caistor road between Capel St Mary and Coddenham (villages named Stratton are almost always situated on Roman roads). It is interesting to note that very few Anglo-Saxon artefacts have been found on the Shotley peninsula, on the opposite side of the Orwell to Stratton. This is, of course, part of the exclusion zone in Essex (see Map 9 on page 138: area C), but it is also possible that Medraut wished to avoid any threat from the south to either his headquarters or the road leading to Walton Castle. This would have left him free to direct maximum attention to the greater threat from north of the Deben.

Medraut's route to the northern fringe of the exclusion zone would then have followed the Stour valley west to its headwaters in the East Anglian highlands. Here another Roman road leads further west to Grantchester and thence to either Peterborough or Leicester. Along the whole of this route, the land had been cleared of Anglo-Saxon settlements. The advantages of leaving Medraut in control at Walton were obvious, and Arthur, by making such a disposition, would have underlined the personal confidence he placed in Medraut's loyalty and military competence.

In the meantime, Arthur would have been left free to withdraw his main force to South Cadbury, to regroup and to consolidate his control of the west and centre of the island. There are records of British leaders undertaking campaigns in the west to eliminate the power of the Irish dynasties from that part of Britain now known as Wales. They had spread their control inland from the west coast in the fifth century. The campaigns in Wales led by Catwallaun Longhand and Agricola mentioned earlier can probably be dated to the period following the establishment of the East Anglian Marches.

There is, however, little hint of a return to prosperity or any sort of revival of a Roman-type civilization during the period after the East

Anglian campaign. Writing from his own experience, about 20 years after Arthur's death, Gildas admits only to some partial recovery from the destruction caused by the wars which occupied most of the second half of the fifth century. He denies complete recovery, particularly of the towns and cities. A structured countryside economy had progressively vanished as the Roman villas were destroyed or abandoned, and the subsequent agricultural economy must have been adversely affected by the almost continual warfare which followed. Agricultural skills must have been lost and, equally importantly, since the towns had not been rebuilt, craft skills must have evaporated.

In political terms, the gap between Badon in 496 and Camlann in 517 is filled by the expulsion of the Irish dynasties from the West Country, by Arthur's continuing control of south-coast Saxon incursions and by Medraut's control of the East Anglian and Lincolnshire bridgeheads. These 20 years are the time in which Arthur no doubt hoped to reconstruct the land after the long campaigns and bitter struggles between invader and defender from 440 to the early years of the sixth century. During the whole of this period there is, however, no record of any expulsion of the invaders from Britain. At the same time, there is also no record of the invading forces making any progress further inland.

According to *The Anglo-Saxon Chronicle,* this period also coincides with the early stages of the West Saxon invasion campaign, as described in Chapter 6. Cerdic, it will be remembered, after coming to some arrangement with the invading Saxons, scored his first victory at Netley in 508, only a few kilometres inland from the invasion landing point. Up to the date of Camlann in 517, he had made no further progress and met the British only two years later in an inconclusive engagement at Charford, about 16 kilometres (ten miles) from Netley. An uncertain advance of little more than 16 kilometres in the gap between Badon and Camlann says much for Arthur's defence and little for the military ability of the invaders.

In spite of Arthur's political and military successes, his hopes for reconstruction could not be realized. This becomes clear from the gloomy view Gildas takes of the condition of Britain in 540, some 20 years after Arthur's death. He attacks the morals and conduct of five West Country kings. He castigates them as tyrants who plundered and terrorized their subjects and individually led most immoral lives. In the text there is, around 540, no indication of any central authority, no High King who could exercise reasonable control over local rulers, but rather a growth of capricious and unpredictable petty kings. It is very possible that this process of disintegration started after Arthur's death at the battle of Camlann, which put an end to any hope of complete British recovery. It is therefore important to examine the events which may have led up to the disaster of Arthur's final battle.

It is generally accepted by historians that the battle of Badon is the most important victory of the British at the time of the Anglo-Saxon settlements, in view of the delay it imposed on the progress of the conquest. It will be argued here, however, that it was the consequences of the two battles of Badon and Camlann, taken together, which were instrumental both in confirming the historical importance of Arthur and also in setting the scene for the development of Britain into England.

The report of the battle of Camlann in the *Annales Cambriae* includes the death of Arthur and Medraut but does not say explicitly whether or not they were on opposing sides. There would, however, be little cause to mention Medraut at all if he was on Arthur's side. The site of the battle is obscure and its location is not helped by the fact that the entry does not name the enemy, but there is little doubt that Arthur's opponents were the Anglo-Saxons. The main economic and social centre of Britain lay south of the Humber both before and after the Roman departure – the best agricultural land was in the south, the main trading contacts with the Continent were in the south – and the chief invasion pressures also lay to south and east, although there was secondary pressure from the Irish in the west. Apart from the two Arthurian battles in Scotland, which were probably only a matter of 'showing the flag', there had been no indication of danger coming from the north. For all these reasons, one attempt to identify Camlann with Camboglanna, the Roman fort of Birdoswald on Hadrian's Wall, using philology alone, cannot be easily sustained.

Another reason for excluding any location of Camlann in the north arises from the new military situation in the south. A man such as Arthur, capable of planning the strategy of the Badon campaign and executing the tactics of the several different battle situations, would never have taken his main forces so far north when his main supply base and the urgent threats to his kingdom lay far to the south. He moved north of the Wash in the Badon campaign only in the sure knowledge that Ambrosius remained behind to secure the south during his absence. Pressure from the invaders had increased since Badon. Medraut was fully engaged in East Anglia and could not be left to hold the whole of the south, as Ambrosius had been.

Indeed, the political situation in the east constituted an unexpected source of danger to Arthur. This danger originated in the man Arthur had chosen as his viceroy, Medraut, who was holding the barrier against Anglo-Saxon expansion in East Anglia from his fort at Walton Castle. Medraut would have had every opportunity, through proximity and perhaps inclination, to establish first friendly and then close relationships with the very people he was expected to restrain. With his position as something more than a king in the east, and being so far from South Cadbury, it would have been a great temptation to attempt to mount a coalition between his forces and the East Anglian invaders with the intention of taking Arthur's place as High King. In this he would be following the same plan of forming an alliance with the enemy which was adopted by Cerdic when the West Saxons landed on the south coast. He would also be following the Celtic tendency of being willing to form an alliance with a foreign nation in order to defeat people of his own race. Perhaps some memory of this alliance lingered in the west, for Geoffrey of Monmouth used it in his imaginary history published some six centuries later; it certainly provides a reasonable explanation for the causes of the battle of Camlann.

If Medraut did decide to form an alliance with the Angles and move westwards against Arthur, it would mean that the opposing forces probably met somewhere on a line linking Ipswich to South Cadbury. The name Camlann does not help very much in deciding the location of the battle. In translation it means 'crooked valley' and there are many such in the Chilterns, the Downs and the Cotswolds. The Goring Gap, through which the Thames flows south between the Chiltern Hills, is a particularly good example. In fact, a concentration of weapons which can be approximately dated to this period has been found in the Thames in this area.

It is possible that Arthur had received information of Medraut's treachery and was moving east to meet the threat (see Map 11 on page 151). He could have taken his forces eastwards from South Cadbury along the Roman road system to Silchester and then north, where the road runs through the Goring Gap, or, alternatively, he could have advanced east along the Icknield Way to the place where it crosses the Thames in the Goring Gap. In either case, he would have been following the route he had taken some 20 years earlier towards his campaign in East Anglia following the victory at Badon Hill. In the Goring Gap he could well have encountered Medraut leading a combined British–Anglo-Saxon force advancing west along the Icknield Way from East Anglia, towards the centre of Arthur's power at South Cadbury. The outcome in the battle of the 'crooked valley' had a profound effect on the future of the country, although it was not recorded in the *Annales Cambriae* as either a victory or a defeat for one side or the other.

Arthur's death at Camlann put an end not only to his strategic plans but also to any hope there may have been of restoring the prosperity of Britain. In addition, the death of Medraut deprived Britain of the only man who might possibly have succeeded Arthur as High King. After nearly 50 years under the unifying influence first of Ambrosius Aurelianus and then of Arthur, there is no subsequent record of any High King or any centre of power in Britain. There was, as Gildas has described, only growing evidence of British fragmentation and degeneration.

There is one paragraph in Gildas which, as well as illustrating the general deterioration in Britain, shows how a petty king who may have had links with Arthur is providing a very inferior form of leadership. One of the five kings who are specifically targeted by Gildas is described as 'a despiser of God'. This man, named Cuneglasus, is also referred to as 'the driver of the chariot of the bear's stronghold'. This may be an oblique reference to Arthur, as the word for 'bear' in Celtic is '*arth*'. That a charioteer has become king, and an evil one at that, is a measure of the depth to which Gildas believes Britain has fallen.

Although both leaders died at Camlann, it is very possible that, at the end of the engagement, the advantage lay with the British forces led by Arthur. The evidence for this conclusion lies in *The Anglo-Saxon*

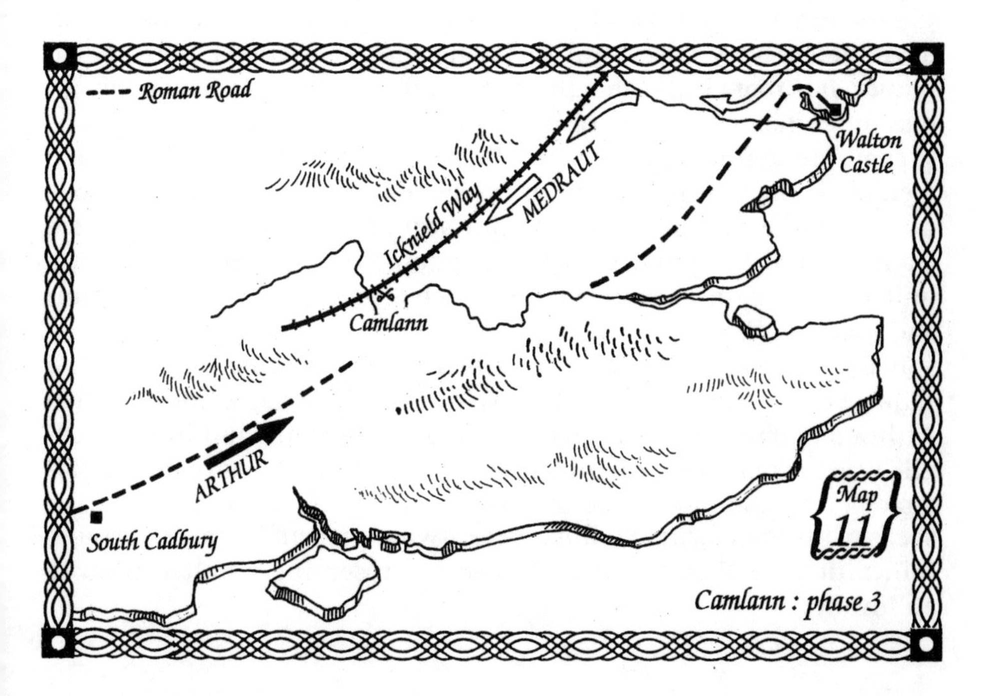

Camlann : phase 3

*Chronicle*. Here, although no explicit information is provided on Camlann, there is a clear picture of the very slow rate of advance of the invaders over many subsequent years. Taking the date of Camlann as 517, Cerdic's conflict at Charford in 519 was inconclusive and so was the battle at 'Cerdic's-ley' in 527. The first unequivocal mainland victory for the West Saxons, following the defeat of the British King Natanleod at Netley in 508, did not occur until Cynric took Salisbury in 552, 35 years after Camlann. Additional evidence of the British advantage after Camlann comes from the East Anglian record in *The Anglo-Saxon Chronicle*, where it is recorded that the final Anglian breakout under Cuthulf did not occur until 571. This evidence suggests that the Angles, after Camlann, retreated back to their bridgehead in the east.

The influence of Arthur's military reputation must have persisted long after Camlann, but the deterioration of the British leaders, castigated by Gildas, in the end hastened the series of Anglo-Saxon victories from 552 onwards. The Anglian breakout in 571 led to the victories of Cuthulf at Bedford and in Oxfordshire and was quickly followed on by Ceawlin's conquest of large areas in the west of the country.

The final failure of the British, in spite of the time-lag due to the lingering influence of Arthur's reputation, cannot, however, be totally ascribed to the deteriorating morals of the British kings. After all, Clovis and his Merovingian successors were equally immoral but nevertheless very successful in laying the foundations of medieval France. It is more likely that the cause of the final Anglo-Saxon victory was the endemic Celtic inability, in the absence of exceptional leaders, to combine against an enemy. To rise to the occasion, it always needed men or women of the calibre of Cassivellaunus, Vercingetorix, Boudicca or, indeed, Ambrosius, Arthur and Medraut. Only under such leaders could the separate petty kingdoms be inspired to present a united front against the invader. No such leader appeared after Arthur and Medraut died.

If the sequence of events described here is accepted, and such a sequence is certainly consistent with the historical evidence, then Arthur's misjudgement in placing Medraut in command in East Anglia was the main factor in precipitating the final success of the Anglo-Saxons towards the end of the sixth century. At the same time, the seeds of ultimate British failure were always present in the underlying difficulties the Celts perpetually had in presenting a united front to an invader.

# CHAPTER 9

# Arthur's Legacy

AT THE outset of the book it had to be acknowledged that there was doubt about Arthur's very existence and, even if existence was conceded, much uncertainty as to his importance and a complete lack of any personal details. The situation with regard to his immediate predecessor, Ambrosius Aurelianus, was very similar. According to Gildas, Ambrosius was 'a gentleman who, perhaps alone of the Romans, had survived the shock of the notable storm' – that is, the first Anglo-Saxon drive to the west. In Nennius, apart from an apocryphal myth relating to the boy Ambrosius, there is only a single mention of Ambrosius as the High King. There was, however, relatively firm documentation of some of Arthur's military achievements, which have been shown to be consistent with a very reasonable historical sequence. Consequently, these achievements permit some personal details to be deduced.

Arthur was a capable military commander – witness his victories. He chose his command to consist chiefly, if not totally, of light cavalry formations. By good fortune, or more probably as a result of his knowledge of the men under his command, this type of unit fitted well with the temperament of the kings and warriors of the Celtic tribes. Arthur's success clearly showed that he made full use of the knowledge he possessed as a result of his mixed Roman and Celtic background and experience. In particular, he held positions which were directly related to both these backgrounds. First, as leader of the kings of Britain in battle, he inherited the Celtic mantle of Cassivellaunus, Caratacus and Boudicca. Second, as the only possible successor of Ambrosius, he was the Celtic High King of Britain. Finally, with the title of 'emperor' in 'The Elegy to Geraint', he was the last in line of the Romans who, from Britain, aspired to imperial status, following the examples of Albinus, Carausius, Constantine the Great, Magnus Maximus and Constantine III.

On the basis of human life expectancy and from information and dating in Gildas, Nennius, the *Annales Cambriae* and *The Anglo-Saxon Chronicle*, it is almost certain that Ambrosius Aurelianus died in the last decade of the fifth century. Consequently, Arthur held effective command from the middle or end of the Badon campaign almost to the end of the second decade of the sixth century.

His predominating influence in Britain stretched from his first campaign, which may have started as early as 490, to his death around 517. This period was of about the same length as Ambrosius's tenure as High King from about 470 to some time between 490 and 495. Although there is no documentary proof, it is almost certain that Arthur held the rank of High King for more than 20 years. Such a position, held for so long in such violent times, must be evidence of high intelligence, a logical mind and substantial military ability. In spite of these qualities, Arthur did not solve the problem posed by the failure of cavalry (without stirrups) facing linear earthworks.

Unfortunately, the failure of archaeology to uncover direct and unequivocal evidence for the sites of Arthur's birth, his headquarters or his burial place left the four main documentary sources alone in support of his existence. Although they did just that, the Arthurian military successes they recorded had to be set against the inescapable fact that, in the end, the Anglo-Saxons prevailed and the British, Arthur's people, were driven into the western fringes of the island. This ultimate conclusion to Arthur's attempts to preserve the British state would seem to suggest that, in spite of his military prowess, he completely failed in his objectives. The Arthurian interlude would, then, amount to an unimportant episode in the inevitable collapse of the western Roman Empire and its replacement by the medieval nation states of western Europe.

Another factor was, however, introduced in the search for some greater impact that Arthur may have made on the history of this island. This new factor resulted from a comparison between the conquest of two similar dioceses of the western Roman Empire by two similar tribes, or groups of tribes, from north-western Europe. The Anglo-Saxons attacked Britain and the Franks attacked Gaul. This comparison was made on a generally accepted 'broad-brush' overview of the history of the period.

The comparison between Britain and Gaul centred upon these two noteworthy invasion sequences. In spite of similarities at the outset, substantial differences appeared during the sequences and at their end, when the Anglo-Saxons and the Franks respectively took control of England and France. In the first place, the conquest of each diocese by similar Germanic tribes took just less than 30 years in Gaul (481 to 509), compared with one and a half centuries (446 to 593) in Britain. In order to emphasize the great difference in the timescale of the invasions in Gaul and Britain, a dated sequence of events is provided in Appendices 1 and 2.

In addition to differences in the overall duration, there were substantial differences in the ways England and France developed after the conquests were completed. These differences appeared in the fields of language, law and social structure and were, together with the duration factor, clearly linked to the military abilities of the agressor, Clovis, in Gaul, and in Britain to the abilities of the defenders, Vortimer, Ambrosius and, above all, Arthur.

It is possible to assess the relative influence of these three British leaders. Vortimer was the first to turn the tide against the invader, but an early death ended his career prematurely. Ambrosius held the invaders at bay during the later years of his life, winning some, but not all battles and establishing recruitment sites round the periphery of his country. Arthur, however, put the seal on a British recovery, which was ensured by the aggressive and victorious campaign which ended at the battle of Badon. This campaign was more decisive and successful than any of the battles fought by Ambrosius. Nevertheless, like Ambrosius, Arthur failed to eject the invaders from Britain in a probable East Anglian campaign after the Badon battle. This second campaign probably foundered in battles on the linear earthworks built by the Anglo-Saxons on the Icknield Way just south of Cambridge. The failure may well have been due to British over-reliance on light cavalry without stirrups and a corresponding neglect of infantry. It may also have been due to Anglo-Saxon skill in the building and utilization of linear earthworks. However, although the campaign failed and consequently is not remembered in bardic poetry, there is evidence that Arthur did execute a successful plan to contain his main enemies in East Anglia. Even so, he chose the wrong man to leave in charge of the eastern Marches.

The substitution of a containment policy with Medraut in charge is a deduction which owes much to the researches of Morris and Rigold. The appointment of Medraut initiated the final phase of Arthur's reign. Following the example of many Celtic leaders before him, Medraut could well have succumbed to the temptation to form an alliance with the tribe he was supposed to contain, and to challenge Arthur's position as High King. If this was the case, Camlann is probably located in a valley in the Chilterns, possibly the Goring Gap, in a direct line between Walton and South Cadbury. Medraut's treason and insurrection, followed by Camlann, terminated Arthur's quarter-century reign as High King. It also terminated any future possibility of final victory against the invaders, for there was no leader left who could unite the Celtic tribes against them. This situation proved to be quite crucial to the whole problem of Arthur's legacy to history.

After the defeat of Medraut at Camlann, and both his and Arthur's deaths, the Angles returned to their bridgehead and there is no evidence of further aggression from that direction until the break-out led by Cuthulf in 571. The whole conquest sequence made little progress until the battle of Salisbury in 552, possibly due to the fading influence of Arthur and to the gradual decay in British leadership without the guidance of a High King. The disappearance of effective British leadership following Camlann was paralleled by economic and cultural deterioration, which resulted in an ever-increasing rate of Anglo-Saxon victories. These persisted until the invaders reached the boundaries of Wales and there they halted. The state of the conquered land of Britain displayed no attractive alternative culture for the Anglo-Saxons to adopt, modify or change. This situation was in complete contrast with the way the Franks adopted, modified and changed the Gallic culture they found relatively undisturbed after the rapid victories of Clovis. In the end, however, the success of the invaders was as complete in Britain as it had been in Gaul almost a century earlier. Clovis became master of France and Ceawlin, and after him Aethelbert, became Bretwaldas of England.

The arguments presented and summarized here lead to a surprising and somewhat ironic conclusion that initial great success had ended in final complete collapse. The subsequent British failures and mistakes led to almost complete elimination of Arthur's people from the major part of Britain. By their stubborn and successful opposition, Ambrosius and Arthur had held the invaders in check for many years. However, the effort they made involved a decay in the social structure and wealth of the land. After the the death of Arthur in Medraut's treasonable attack, there was no successor capable of restoration or continued resistance to an equally stubborn invader. The economic prosperity of the island had been destroyed and the decay and fragmentation so well described by Gildas continued until all the British leaders up to the borders of the West Country, Wales and Cumbria had been defeated.

Consequently, the victory of the Anglo-Saxons in the second half of the sixth century found a social and military vacuum quite unlike the lively structures which Clovis encountered after his relatively swift campaigns and which he could modify or absorb. The exhaustion of the country, the failure to eject the invaders from East Anglia, the treachery of Medraut and the lack of a successor High King were in the end the causes of the development of a culture quite different from that which developed in Gaul. Thus, in spite of both conquests being achieved by tribes from north-western Europe, Anglo-Saxon language and law prevailed only in England. In France the language and law of the Franks were largely replaced by Roman equivalents. England became an Anglo-Saxon country; France became an amalgam of Celtic, Roman and Frankish peoples.

This result was a consequence of the abilities of the leaders. If any Anglo-Saxon leader had been as ruthless and efficient as Clovis, and if Ambrosius and Arthur had been as ineffectual as Syagrius, it is just possible that England would have developed into a country similar to France. In that case, we would be speaking a Romance language and our legal system would be based on the Roman model.

This did not happen and Arthur's legacy to history can only be linked to the actual outcome based on relative British success between about 465 and 517 and British collapse thereafter. As a consequence, the Anglo-Saxon way of life in England, unlike the Frankish way in Gaul, was left to develop in comparative isolation, largely uninfluenced by Roman language, law and customs. In a similar manner, the Celtic way of life in Wales was equally isolated for a similar period of time and it was there that Arthur's own people developed their unique individuality.

As a result, two very different states were left in Britain. The first, although not yet politically homogeneous, was by far the larger and was predominantly Anglo-Saxon. The second comprised the land which became the residual Celtic state of Wales. This creation of two states, unequal in size, each with homogeneous but very different cultures, was Arthur's legacy to history.

The importance of this legacy is a matter of recorded history. After the final success of their conquest, the Anglo-Saxons contained those British falling within the Welsh boundaries, just as they themselves had been contained by the East Anglian Marches established by Arthur and held by Medraut in the late fifth and early sixth centuries. The new cordon was finally sealed in the eighth century, when Offa, King of Mercia, built his great earthwork stretching from north to south Wales. Behind Offa's Dyke the British became the Welsh and developed the great culture of Wales, with its strong tradition of poetry and song. The Welsh maintained their independence until Edward I united Wales with England in 1295. They never lost their identity, however, and as late as 1405 the Welsh prince, Owen Glendower, was claiming independence, only to be defeated by Prince Henry (later Henry V). In even later years, the Welsh Tudors regained control of England when Henry Tudor defeated Richard III at Bosworth Field to become Henry VII, and in modern times the Welsh supplied one of the greatest prime ministers to the United Kingdom in the person of David Lloyd George. It has, of course, needed a continuous effort on the part of the Welsh to maintain their identity in the face of their larger neighbour. However, no one can doubt after reading Professor Gwyn Williams' book, *When Was Wales,* that Arthur's people and their language will survive and prosper.

On the other hand, the residual British, left behind in eastern and central Britain (or England, as the land had now become) after the defeat of their military leaders, did not retain their identity. They quickly adopted Anglo-Saxon ways, lost their language and integrated with their conquerors.

The Anglo-Saxon way of life developed over the next five centuries almost unaffected by two subsequent invasions, the Viking (793–876) and the Danish (1016–42). In these invasions the aggressors were of a similar ethnic background and caused little change to English customs. The Norman invaders in 1066 did introduce Continental influences, but these were eventually absorbed into English life.

Thus there is a direct and consequential link between the intervention of Arthur and the unique development of both Anglo-Saxon and Welsh cultures, whereas the complete success of Clovis across the Channel led to a blending of Romano-Celtic and Teutonic cultures, in strong contrast with the two independent cultures in Britain. Arthur ensured the survival of the Brythonic Celtic language and, although he probably never spoke an Anglo-Saxon word, he could also be regarded as the father both of the Anglo-Saxon language, which became English, and of England.

The inhabitants of this land are, however, no longer pure Anglo-Saxon, if ever such a race existed. There have been many immigrants over the centuries who have stayed and are now, once again, all described as British. These include the English descendants of the original Anglo-Saxon, Viking and Danish invaders, the descendants of the original British in the western fringes of the island, the Normans, the Scots, some of the Irish and the many immigrants from Europe and the Commonwealth. Because of the multiracial origins of the peoples of this island, it is not so important for Arthur to be described as the father of England. His importance lies rather in the fact that his intervention permitted the development of the culture, ideas and ideals of two peoples: his own people, the present inhabitants of Wales, and also the adventurous tribes who crossed the North Sea in those early centuries, both of whom were allowed to develop without much external influence for almost 500 years.

During this long time, patterns of national behaviour were set in England by the Anglo-Saxons and adopted, without major modification, by subsequent immigrants. These patterns have made a unique impact on the world scene. They have influenced the growth of parliamentary institutions, the colonization of North America, the subsequent Declaration of Independence by the United States and the growth of the British Empire, together with its translation into the Commonwealth. The language spoken by the Anglo-Saxons has developed into modern English, which has become a world language. There are more people who use English as a second language than speak it as a native tongue. It is used by air and sea traffic round the globe and by almost all scientists reporting their work internationally. In addition, Anglo-Saxon law has provided the 'common law' foundation for many countries round the world.

The intervention of Arthur, the last of the three High Kings of Britain, provided the trigger which set all these developments in train. Herein lies his unique importance. Rather than being remembered as the hero king of a delightful legend, he should be remembered, as William of Malmesbury might have wished, as a man who changed the course of the history of the world. By his intervention and bitter struggle, Britain south of Hadrian's Wall was cleared for the development of two separate nations with very different cultures. The larger of these, the English nation, was enabled to develop in unique isolation for half a millennium, and thereby to set a world pattern and to create a world language.

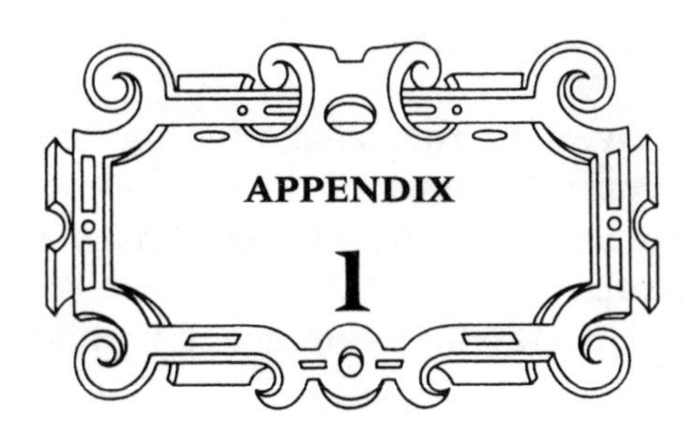


# Table of Events in Gaul

| | |
|---|---|
| 435–6 | Aetius defeats the Burgundian and Frankish invasion of Gaul |
| 446 | British appeal to Aetius for help rejected due to the growing danger from Attila's westward advance |
| 451 | Aetius causes Attila to withdraw from Gaul after the battle near Châlons-sur-Marne |
| 454 | Aetius dies |
| 455–6 | Avitus appoints Aegidius as *magister militum* in northern Gaul |
| 456–64 | Aegidius creates the Kingdom of Soissons in northern Gaul |
| 464 | Aegidius dies and Syagrius succeeds to the Kingdom of Soissons |
| 481 | Alliance between the Kingdom of Soissons and the Franks broken by the death of Childeric, a Frankish king; the succession of his son Clovis |
| 481–5 | Clovis becomes pre-eminent among the Frankish tribes |
| 486 | Start of the conquest of Gaul; Clovis defeats Syagrius in a battle near Soissons |
| 491 | Clovis's unsuccessful attack on the Thuringians |
| 493 | Marriage of Clovis and Clotilda |
| 496 | Clovis defeats the Alemanni and is baptized into the Catholic faith |
| 500 | Clovis defeats the Burgundians near Dijon, followed by the unsuccessful siege of Avignon and a subsequent Frankish retreat |

| | |
|---|---|
| 507 | Clovis moves on the Visigoths and defeats Alaric II at Vouillé; control of most of Gaul achieved by Clovis |
| 508–9 | Theodoric recovers Provence for himself and Septimania for the Visigoths |
| 511 | Death of Clovis, who is succeeded by his four sons |

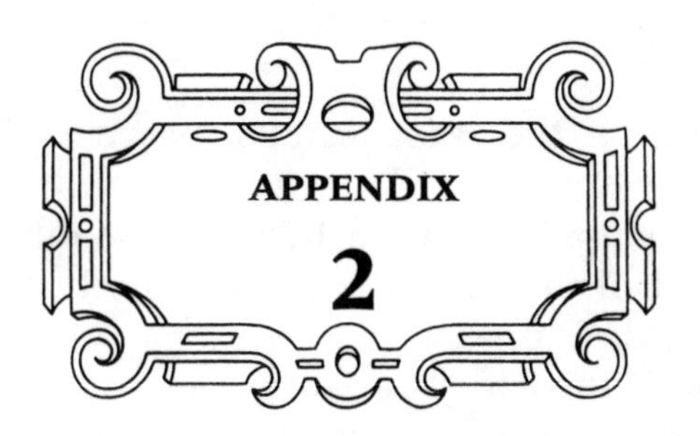

# APPENDIX 2

# Table of Events in Britain

| | |
|---|---|
| 400–410 | Probable birth of Vortigern and the Elder Ambrosius |
| 425 | Accession of Vortigern |
| 428 | First arrival of invaders, led by Hengist |
| 428–40 | Hengist's actions against the Picts |
| 429 | First visit to Britain by St Germanus |
| 430–40 | Probable birth of Vortimer and the Younger Ambrosius (Ambrosius Aurelianus) |
| 437 | Clash between the Elder Ambrosius and Vitalinus (Vortigern?) at Wallop |
| 440 | First major drive to the west by the invaders |
| 440–46 | Emigration of some British to northern Gaul |
| 446 | Appeal to Aetius for help and second visit of St Germanus |
| 437–55 | Probable death of the Elder Ambrosius |
| 446–55 | Gradual recovery under Vortigern and Vortimer |
| 455–65 | Battles between Vortimer and Hengist for the control of Kent, with the latter successful |
| 460–70 | Probable birth of Arthur |
| 465–70 | Probable deaths of Vortigern and Vortimer and the accession of the Younger Ambrosius as High King |
| 470–80 | Establishment of Ambrosius's recruitment sites |
| 477–90 | Landing of the South Saxons at Selsey and Aelle's south-coast campaign |
| 490–93 | Probable start of Arthur's Badon campaign |
| 490–96 | Probable death of Ambrosius and accession of Arthur as High King while on the Badon campaign |

| | |
|---|---|
| 495 | Landing of the West Saxons, probably in Southampton Water |
| 496 | Arthur's final victory at Badon, probably over Aelle, and the end of the Badon campaign; probable end of Aelle's Bretwaldaship |
| 496–517 | Period of British ascendancy |
| 500–510 | Arthur's suggested second assault on the East Anglian bridgehead; success at the Heydon, Flean and Devil's Ditches along the Icknield Way; British held at the Black Ditches and River Lark; clearance of the invaders from the exclusion zone; Medraut left to control the East Anglian Marches from Walton Castle |
| 508 | Cerdic's and the West Saxons' first victory over the British at Netley |
| 517 | Revolt of Medraut, leading a coalition of Anglian invaders and his British supporters against Arthur; battle of Camlann, in which both Arthur and Medraut die |
| 517 | Withdrawal of Angles eastwards |
| 519 | Battle at Charford between Cerdic and the British: inconclusive result |
| 527 | Battle at 'Cerdic's-ley' between Cerdic and the British: inconclusive result |
| 530 | Cerdic captures the Isle of Wight |
| 534 | Cerdic succeeded by Cynric |
| 552 | Cynric defeats the British at Salisbury |
| 556 | Cynric probably defeats the British at Barbury Castle |
| 560 | Cynric succeeded by Ceawlin |
| 568 | Ceawlin repulses Aethelbert's attempt to expand westwards |
| 571 | Cuthulf's breakout from East Anglia, with victories at Bedford and four towns, ending on the upper reaches of the Thames; Cuthulf dies in the same year |
| 577 | Ceawlin's advance westward, with victory at Dyrham and the capture of Gloucester, Cirencester and Bath |
| 584 | Ceawlin's victory at Fretherne |
| 593 | Death of Ceawlin |
| 597 | Arrival of St Augustine in Kent |

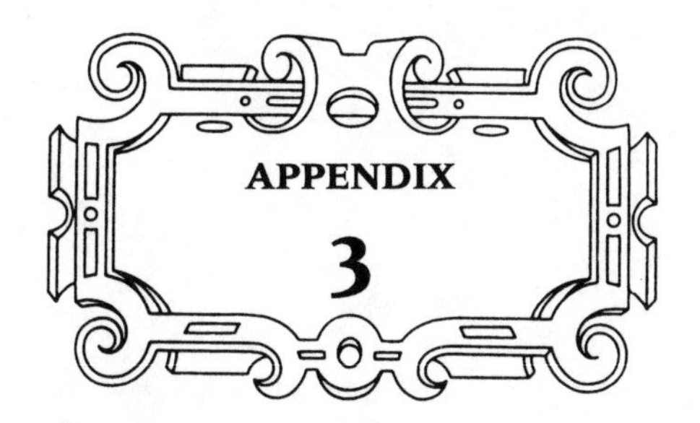

# APPENDIX 3

## Phases of the British Conquest

| | |
|---|---|
| Phase 1, 428–77 | Aggression by Hengist and the first two stages of British recovery under Vortimer and the Younger Ambrosius |
| Phase 2, 477–90 | First attack by the South Saxons contained by Ambrosius |
| Phase 3, 490–517 | Third stage of British recovery under Arthur, achieved in the Badon and East Anglian campaigns; failure to eliminate any of the invaders' bridgeheads in the east and south |
| Phase 4, 495–556 | The West Saxon campaign; confined to the south coast until their victory at Salisbury in 552 |
| Phase 5, 571 | The Anglian breakout under Cuthulf; Angles meet the West Saxons on the Thames |
| Phase 6, 577–84 | Completion of the conquest with Ceawlin's advance westwards |

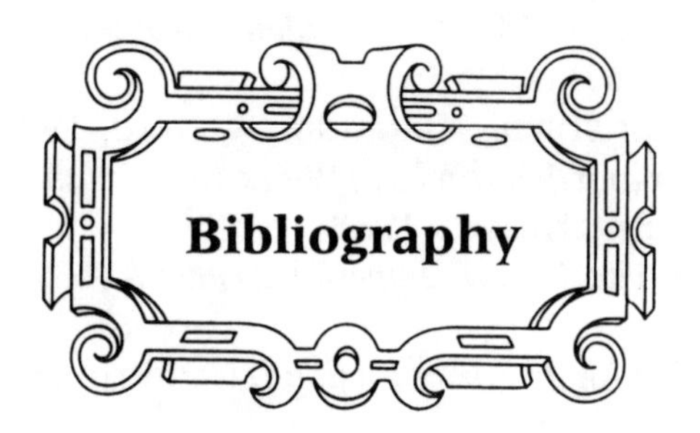

# Bibliography


Alcock, Leslie *Arthur's Britain*, Allen Lane, London, 1971

—— 'Excavations at South Cadbury Castle', *Antiquaries Journal*, Vol. XLVIII, 1968, p. 6

*The Anglo-Saxon Chronicle* Everyman, London, 1912

*Annales Cambriae*, see Nennius

Bede *History of the English Church and People*, Penguin Books, Harmondsworth, 1972

Camden, William *Britannia*, 1607

Frere, Sheppard *Britannia*, Routledge and Kegan Paul, 1987

Funck-Brentano, Father *The National History of France: The Earliest Times*, Heinemann, London, 1927

Geoffrey of Monmouth *History of the Kings of Britain*, Penguin Books, Harmondsworth, 1966

Gildas *On the Ruin of Britain*, Phillimore and Co., London and Chichester, 1978

Giraldus Cambrensis *De Principis Instructione*, *c.* 1193

Gregory of Tours *The History of the Franks*, *c.* 580

Johnson, Stephen *The Roman Forts of the Saxon Shore*, Elek, London, 1976

Leland, John *Assertio Inclytissimi Arturii Regis Britanniae*, 1544

Malory, Thomas *Le Morte d'Arthur*, Penguin Books, Harmondsworth, 1969

Markale, Jean *King Arthur: King of Kings*, Gordon & Cremonesi, 1977

Morris, John *The Age of Arthur*, Weidenfeld and Nicolson, London, 1973

Myres, J. N. L. *The English Settlements*, Clarendon, Oxford, 1986

Nennius *The History of the British* (includes *Annales Cambriae*), Phillimore and Co., London and Chichester, 1980

Radford, C. A. R. 'Tintagel: The Castle and Celtic Monastery', *Antiquaries Journal*, Vol. XV, 1935, p. 401

Rigold, S. E. 'Further Evidence about the Site of Dommoc', *Journal of the British Archaeological Society*, Vol. 37, 1974, p. 97

—— 'The Supposed See of Dunwich', *Journal of the British Archaeological Society*, Vol. 24, 1961, p. 55

Salway, Peter *Roman Britain*, Clarendon, Oxford, 1981

Skene, W. F. *Arthur and the Britons in Wales and Scotland*, edited by Derek Bryce, Llanerch Enterprises, 1988

Webster, Graham *The Roman Imperial Army*, A & C Black, London, 1981

Whitelock, Dorothy *Anglo-Saxon England*, Cambridge University Press, Cambridge, 1972

William of Malmesbury *Gesta Regum*, 1120

Williams, Gwyn A. *When Was Wales*, Penguin Books, Harmondsworth, 1985

# Index